AN ITALIAN RENAISSANCE

CHOOSING LIFE IN CANADA

ROBERT ELI RUBINSTEIN

Foreword by Rabbi Dr. Jacob J. Schacter

URIM PUBLICATIONS
Jerusalem ◆ New York

An Italian Renaissance
Choosing Life in Canada

Text copyright © 2010 Robert Eli Rubinstein

Artwork copyright © 2010 Rochelle Rubinstein
  Printed, painted and carved wood panels
  Cover and first illustration: Details from THE VILLAGE, 2007
  Second illustration: Detail from KADDISH, 2008

Printed in Israel
First Edition

ISBN: 978-965-524-044-3

COVER DESIGN: Shani Schmell
TYPESETTING: Daniella Barak
EDITORIAL AND PRODUCTION DIRECTOR: Daniella Barak
EDITOR: Michael Dekel

Urim Publications, P.O. Box 52287, Jerusalem 91521 Israel

Lambda Publishers Inc.
3709 13th Avenue, Brooklyn, New York 11218 U.S.A.
Tel: 718-972-5449 Fax: 718-972-6307 mh@ejudaica.com

www.UrimPublications.com

In loving memory of

Annie Rubinstein Kohn

Blima Rivka Adel bat Daniel

whose splendid life,
though tragically severed,
exemplified the spirit of Grugliasco.

Judit and Béla Rubinstein on their wedding day.
June 9, 1946
UNRRA Camp No. 17, Grugliasco, Italy

*Every child is indebted to his parents
for the gift of life.*

A commonplace truth, to be sure, endlessly reaffirmed.

*But there are parents for whom
endowing life to their children
is a profound declaration of faith
and an act of soaring courage.*

*And there are children for whom
receiving life from their parents,
though the most unlikely happenstance,
inspires unbounded love and devotion.*

Such are my parents.

And such is their child.

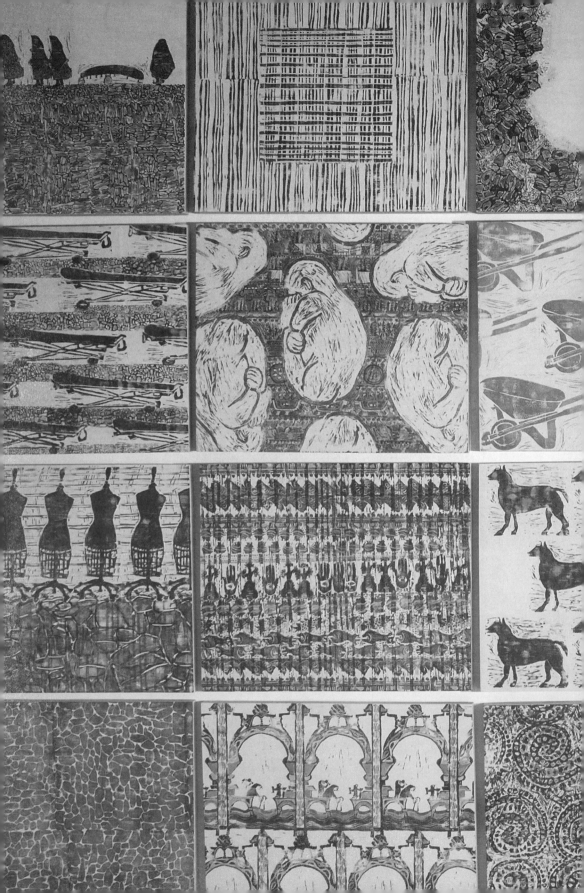

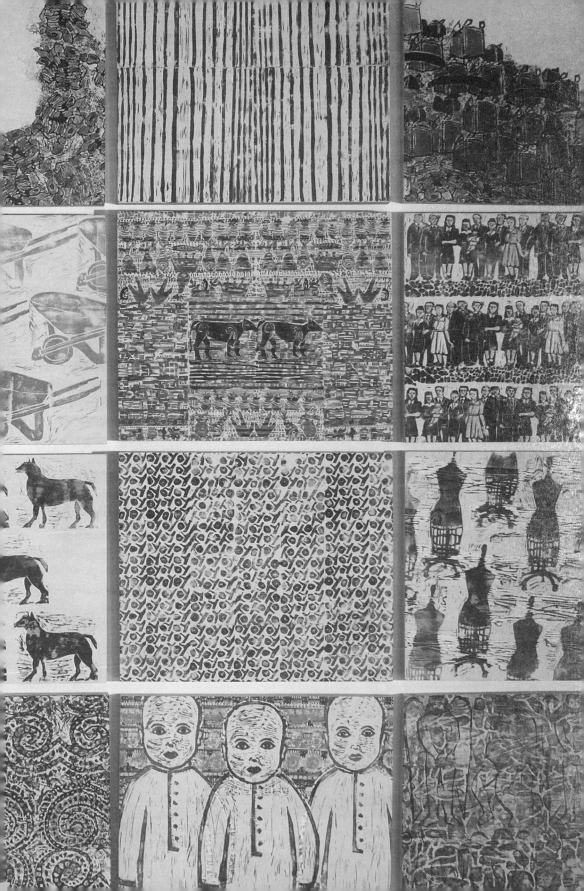

Contents

*Photograph of the family, taken in Grugliasco in the fall of 1947. From left to right:
Armin Rubinstein, Judit Rubinstein, Béla Rubinstein, Magda Zimmerman, David
Zimmerman, Béla Zimmerman, Vera Rubinstein, Dezso Rubinstein, Kicsi Hofstadter
and Sandor Hofstadter.*

FOREWORD

Eli Rubinstein has performed a double *mitzvah* in writing this exceptional book. First, although so much has been written about the Holocaust and its aftermath, many stories remain to be told. In gripping prose, Mr. Rubinstein draws our attention to a little-known post-war refugee camp in the town of Grugliasco near Torino in northwestern Italy, where his Holocaust-survivor parents were married and began to reassemble their shattered lives. He describes the conditions in the camp, and the economic and social challenges its residents had to face. He brings to life one more chapter in the tragic story of the Jewish people in the twentieth century, and for this alone we are in his debt.

But the book is more, much more. It is an extraordinary fulfillment of the biblical commandment to honor one's parents, a sensitive, loving, yet honest testament of a son to his mother and father. I have long been in awe, absolute awe, of Holocaust survivors, witnesses to the utter depravity of humanity at its very worst, and examples of the strength, fortitude, hope and greatness of humanity at its very best. Exposed to the most malignant radiation of human cruelty, they emerged not with fantasies of revenge but with fantasies of respectability and decency. Some of them spoke of their experiences and some did not, but either way, they responded to the total assault of death with an astonishing outpouring of life, and, occasionally, with a stubborn and tenacious commitment to Jewish tradition in the fullest. And, thanks to Mr. Rubinstein's efforts, we can all now number his parents among the best of them. He beautifully describes how, somehow, they were able to emerge from their horrific Holocaust ordeals and live exemplary moral, decent and upstanding lives.

This book is amazing, inspiring, and extraordinarily well written. It is poetic, lyrical, graceful and elegant. It demonstrates remarkable self-awareness and self-reflection. I was unable to put it down and I was deeply moved.

The author writes how his parents were not enthusiastic about contributing to "Holocaust Memorial" projects. "Our children and grand-children are the best memorial to our lost loved ones," they would say. How true this is. Our thanks to Mr. Rubinstein for writing this book, and for the way he wrote it. May God continue to shower His blessings on him and on his remarkable family.

Holocaust Remembrance Day 5769
April 21, 2009
New York, NY

Rabbi Dr. Jacob J. Schacter
University Professor of Jewish History and Jewish Thought
Senior Scholar, Center for the Jewish Future
Yeshiva University

ACKNOWLEDGMENTS

I wish to express my heartfelt appreciation to all those who helped me tell the story of my parents.

My dear sister Rochelle, the talented younger child of our parents, has been profoundly touched, in her own way, by their wartime experiences. Her powerful images provide a striking visual counterpart to my written words.

Mordechai Mandelbaum persuaded my normally taciturn father to reminisce in the presence of a tape recorder. I am grateful to him for thereby securing invaluable information about my father's past which otherwise would have been lost to us forever.

My esteemed teacher at the University of Toronto, Professor Emil Fackenheim of blessed memory, taught me to confront the unparalleled tragedy of the Six Million with both passion and intellectual integrity.

Dr. Daniel Polisar, president of the Shalem Center, urged me early on to convey my parents' remarkable story to a broader audience. His sage suggestions and erudite comments dramatically improved the manuscript.

Rabbi Yitz and Blu Greenberg energized me with their kind words and warm encouragement, and strengthened my resolve to publish this book.

Sara Vinçon's loving reconstruction of the Grugliasco refugee experience had such a deep impact on me that she became a key character in the narrative.

Alvin Abram, Suzanne Balaban, Adam Fuerstenberg, Liebe Geft, Karen Hauser, Carolyn Hessel, Alana Joblin, Anna Porter, Myrna Riback, Haim Rubinstein, Rabbi Jacob J. Schacter, Daniel Septimus, and

Rabbi Yehoshua Weber contributed in various ways to bringing this book to fruition.

My wonderful children, Tamar, Jonathan, Ilan, Dana, Erez, and Hadassa, and my glorious grandchildren, Ikey, Kineret, Max, Ellian, Yishai, Maya, Dov and Daniel, keep me going. A "Sabba-Abba" could not dream of a more devoted fan club.

I could not have completed this undertaking without the steadfast support of my dear wife Renée, herself a child of survivors, who understood how important this project was to me, and loved my parents as her own.

Of course, I bear sole responsibility for any inadvertent errors or inaccuracies in the book. To the extent that my insistence on candor may upset certain people, I express regret, but I offer no apology. One of my father's favorite prayers, *Leolam yehei adam*, recited every morning by traditional Jews, reassures me that I am following the proper path:

> A person should always be God-fearing,
> In private as well as in public,
> Acknowledging the truth,
> And speaking the truth in his heart.

An Italian Renaissance

I am warming up on an elliptical trainer at the Jewish Community Center near my home in Toronto, Canada. The television is tuned to the opening ceremony of the 2006 Winter Olympic Games in *Torino* (Turin), Italy. I find the festive atmosphere, the glowing athletes, and especially the scenes of towering snow-capped peaks, disconcerting. Such things had no place in my virtual Torino of long ago, and for the moment, my thoughts are trapped in the past. I used to imagine the city as endless rows of austere wooden barracks on an interminable plain, teeming with ragged, miserable people. Only when I first visited Torino, many years later, did I become aware of the majestic Italian Alps framing an otherwise rather ordinary European city.

Perspiring profusely on the machine next to me is a well-known Jewish community leader. Seeking relief from the tedium of repetitive exercise, we start to banter about the images on the screen. I mention to my neighbor that although I have never been particularly interested in sporting events, these Olympic Games hold special significance for me because Torino was my birthplace.

When he mutters mild surprise at this fact, I seize the opportunity to explain that I happened to come along while my parents were living in a refugee camp in the neighboring town of Grugliasco. I point out that there were actually a number of such camps in Italy, and that many thousands of traumatized Jewish refugees languished in them after the Second World War as they waited for some country, any country, to take them in.

This is far weightier conversational fare than my neighbor had bargained for after a long day at the office. Groping for an appropriate response, he mumbles that perhaps it is just as well that people do not know much about these places, as they must have been dreadful.

My good judgment fails me, and I do not drop the matter. Such ignorance is regrettable, I proclaim with indignation. Everyone knows about the devastating tragedy that befell the Jews of Europe during the War. It is also widely recognized that many individuals among the surviving remnant were able to rebuild their lives successfully in the years following. But what accounts for this astonishing success? There is a gaping hole in the story of the survivors, between their liberation and their eventual normalization. I believe something quite remarkable happened during the interim period, and people ought to know about it.

I was born in Italy, and my parents were *reborn* in Italy. I grew up regarding the land of my birth as a sort of involuntary sanatorium for my parents, a place where they could convalesce after the horrific ordeals they had endured. Having experienced humankind at its absolute worst, they should by right have despaired of the future. Yet, this is not what happened, thanks in large part to the curative effect of their sojourn in Italy.

Canada became my parents' home after years of dislocation and uncertainty. It was not their destination of choice, any more than Italy had been earlier. Nevertheless, Canada has proved to be a land of great blessing for my family. And while the early years in the new country were challenging, they would have been far more so without the preceding Italian interlude...

Suddenly, I realize that the dialogue has degenerated into a monologue, and an awkward silence ensues. My neighbor and I stare straight ahead at the television set, refocusing attention on the opening ceremony of the Winter Olympic Games.

Choosing Life

I have called heaven and earth today to bear witness against you;
I have set life and death before you, blessing and curse.
Choose life, so that you may live, you and your descendants.
(Deuteronomy 30:19)

When I was a small child, I was afraid to fall asleep at night. I knew that sleeping exposed me to the possibility of being tormented by nightmares. There were several variations of the basic theme. Something big, powerful, and frightening is chasing me. I run with all my might, managing to stay just barely out of its grasp, until I come to a sheer cliff, and then... I wake up screaming.

What was the cause of these nightly torments? I have always resisted the notion that it was anything in the rather mundane experience of my brief life to that point. My struggling immigrant parents did everything in their power to ensure that their child enjoyed the kind of stability and tranquility that had been absent from their own tumultuous lives.

The nightmares simply stopped when I was eight or nine. Since then, I have dreamt regularly, as I understand healthy and well-adjusted people do, but the next morning I can never remember what I dreamt about. I recall reading somewhere that this indicates an introverted personality, which sounds reasonable enough to me, as I have always been very shy.

Yet, I cannot help challenging myself. Is it possible the nightmares were somehow connected to a sensitive boy's intuition that his parents had lived through real-life versions of them? Could their trauma have

3

bled through to his own consciousness and subverted their determined efforts to protect him?

Such a dreary notion makes me profoundly uncomfortable. The implication is that not only the survivors, but their children as well, are doomed to be scarred forever by the wartime tragedy of the Jews of Europe.

It is true that I am the child of two people who suffered greatly before I was born. But I myself never experienced what my parents did. It would be a serious mistake to ignore this crucial point, as some children of survivors do. I refuse to lean on my parents' background as an emotional crutch, as an excuse for any kind of weakness or dysfunction. Doing so would not only be fraudulent, it would be handing an easy victory to the enemy, and this is forbidden to me as the child of my parents.

I have no way of knowing whether my father suffered nightmares like mine when he was a child. He never talked about his life before the War. I do know, however, that as long as I can remember, he suffered terrible nightmares that caused him to moan and wail in his sleep. The next morning, he remembered nothing. By day, my father was strong and resolute, yet upright and compassionate, by all accounts an admirable human being. By night, the forces of darkness temporarily took charge.

My mother, on the other hand, suffers from insomnia, so that she has little time for dreams of any kind. I certainly do not recall her ever experiencing the type of nightmares that plagued my father. I think this is because her inner turmoil finds a healthy outlet during her waking hours; quite the opposite of my father, she feels a powerful need to bear witness to the past, not to express bitterness or vengefulness, but to look confidently toward the future. She speaks and writes passionately about her wartime experiences and the lessons to be drawn about the evils of intolerance. She welcomes the opportunity to address Jews and non-Jews alike, and she takes special pleasure in speaking to young people, in whose hands rests the potential to mould the future. However, no pleasure compares to that of interacting with her grandchildren and great-grandchildren, the living embodiment of her personal triumph.

On occasion, people who are aware of my parents' background marvel that they could be such lovely people. What they really mean, but are too polite to articulate, is that those who had been dragged to the depths of dehumanization might quite naturally be expected to have emerged nasty, devious, and antisocial. In the years following the end of the War, many long-time Canadians refused to fraternize with the European new-comers in their midst. Part of this was, no doubt, the usual snobbish prejudice against poor immigrants. But there was a far more disturbing aspect to it. Decent folk could not help but wonder what the Nazis did with the women. And who could even imagine what the men had to do to stay alive?

The worst – that is, the fittest – survived, the best all died.[1]

This is the disquieting view of Primo Levi, himself a survivor of Aus chwitz, and widely respected as one of the most powerful writers on the tragedy of European Jewry. Levi is mistaken: He himself was one of the best, and *he* survived, so clearly there were exceptions to his rule.

In one of my earliest childhood memories, it is morning, and I am sitting with my adult relatives in the living room of an apartment at the back of a store. Every time the bell rings, someone gets up and goes out front. The only person missing is my father. When I ask my mother where he is, she tells me he had to go somewhere and would be back soon. I am curious to see what is going on out front, but my mother tells me I must stay in the living room. When my father returns, he exchanges silent glances with the others. My parents and I go upstairs to our own apartment. I am too young to understand what it all means.

In another reminiscence from the remote past, I am lying wide-awake, fearful of the nightmares waiting to pounce on me as soon as I fall asleep. (Well aware that I do not like being in the dark, my parents have left the bedroom door slightly ajar to let some light in). The adults are talking in the next room, the only other room in the gloomy little apartment. The only member of the group who never joins in the conversation is my father. I strain to listen, but although I understand the words, the conversation makes no sense to me. Two phrases recur repeatedly as the adults speak: *a haboru elot, a haboru utan.* (Before the war, after the war.) *What war are they talking about, and why is it so important to them?* The adults discuss people I do not know, living in places unfamiliar to me. So it goes, night after night. Eventually, exhaustion overwhelms me and I surrender to sleep.

During the early years of my life, I did not think there was anything out of the ordinary about this. Living in my sheltered little world, it never occurred to me that perhaps my parents' past rendered me different from other children. To the extent that I *did* feel different, I believed it was because my parents were immigrants. Like all children, I craved peer acceptance, and because of my extreme bashfulness, I was mortified at the prospect of standing out from the crowd.

When I started attending kindergarten, I encountered "Canadian" children for the first time, and I realized that the language of the adults in my life was not the language that everyone else spoke. Within a matter of weeks, I was able to converse in English. From that point on, I refused to speak Hungarian any more. This suited my parents just fine: they wanted their child to master the language of their adopted land, and they were eager to learn it themselves. Working hard as they did in those early days, and in the absence of social contacts with non-immigrants, they simply lacked opportunities to learn English. My parents were pleased to welcome me as their first English teacher.

This initial exposure to the "normal" world beyond my family's narrow immigrant circle triggered an uncomfortable tension in me. I was in awe of grownups who spoke perfect, unaccented English, and as much as I loved my parents, it was a source of embarrassment to me that they spoke grammatically flawed and odd-sounding English. When it came to homework, my parents were no help at all, although my mother did try her best.

I remember being envious of schoolmates with Canadian-born parents, who, attuned to popular culture, understood their children's need to wear Davy Crockett hats and Mouseketeer ears, and to play with yo-yos and hula hoops. On account of both the no-nonsense values of their upbringing and the practical necessity of focusing on livelihood, my parents had no concept of leisure-time activity. We did not own a television set. Whenever my classmates discussed the highlights of the previous evening's TV shows at lunchtime, I sat dumbly disconnected.

When I was eight years old, my ever-resourceful mother, a seamstress by trade, decided to sew me a new winter coat. She found a reasonably priced brown tweed remnant at the dressmaker's supply shop, and set about sewing the new coat in her limited spare time. She was disappointed at my lack of enthusiasm when the coat was finally ready. I wore it to school with a deep sense of dread. Sure enough, my worst fears were realized when the other children mocked me mercilessly. Returning home that day, I declared my refusal to wear the coat to school again. I wanted one of those bright blue or red nylon ski jackets from the Eaton's department store that all the other kids wore. Within a few days, my mother relented and took me to Eaton's. I have no idea what happened to the brown tweed coat. Perhaps it ended up being worn by some hapless immigrant child with parents less yielding than mine.

The realization that I was significantly different from the other children, beyond the fact that my parents were struggling immigrants, came one day when I was ten years old. I was with my cousin Shimon, who was visiting Toronto from New York. Our conversation was characteristic of boys that age: When Shimon realized that he knew something I did not, he was only too happy to show off his knowledge. He told me that a man named Hitler and his followers, the Nazis, had killed most of the family. I was dumbfounded. Why would anyone do such a terrible thing, and what could the members of my family possibly have done to deserve such a horrific fate? Of course, I had no answers, but certain things began to make sense. For example, from a tender age I had been aware that Canadian children typically had grandparents, while I did not. Now, thanks to Shimon, I understood why.

I did not dwell on my discovery, nor did I discuss it with anyone. I learned many years later that this was in keeping with the near-universal conspiracy of silence in those days regarding the tragedy of the Jews in Europe. For a long time to come, it would not be a suitable topic to raise in polite company.

I received confirmation of Shimon's unsettling story from an authoritative adult two years later. One day, our Hebrew teacher made a dramatic announcement in class: Adolph Eichmann had been kidnapped by Israeli agents in Argentina and brought to Israel for trial. There were no regular studies that day. Together with my classmates, I listened with rapt attention to the story of how this evil man had devoted himself, efficiently and single-mindedly, to transporting the Jews of Hungary to the death camps, even though it was already clear that Germany was losing the war. I was introduced for the first time to the number Six Million, the enormity of which was beyond grasping. *Hungary? Wasn't that the country my parents came from?* The teacher was talking about my own grandparents, my uncles, aunts, and cousins, only multiplied many times over.

The teacher corroborated what I had learned from Shimon's juvenile boast. The shadowy, ghost-like family I had never known suddenly became vivid and acquired a context. In my mind's eye, I visualized each individual. With exacting detail, I reconstructed in a special corner of my brain an alternate reality populated by my lost relatives. Each of them had a fully developed personality and they were bound to one another by a web of relationships, just as in the normal Canadian families I saw around me.

Parallel to this imaginary universe, a very different and decidedly unwholesome one took form. I started to fantasize about taking revenge on Eichmann. I imagined that I would have him all to myself in a small room without windows or doors. The once mighty monster lay powerless on the floor, his arms and legs bound. I conjured up a sequence of slow, excruciating tortures that I administered to my helpless prisoner. Much as I wanted him to die an agonizing death, my mind kept pushing off the final moment. I understood, deep down, that there could be no finality: Nothing could ever make amends for Eichmann's horrific crimes against the Jewish people.

Much later, my mother told me that she harbored similar fantasies after the War, when she learned what the Nazis had done to her family. In an all-consuming obsession, she thought constantly about avenging her loved ones. After a while, she was alarmed to realize that her compulsion to destroy the murderers was threatening to destroy her instead. Throughout the time she had been in Auschwitz, she was able to preserve her morale and her sense of human dignity. All the attempts to degrade her had failed because in her heart she knew she was morally superior to her tormentors.

My mother resolved to regain the ethical high ground. She had not outlasted her enemies only to sink to their debased level now that she was finally free of them. The anger drained out of her. From that point on, she did not hate the Germans or their many accomplices, although she could never forget what they had done. She diverted her energies to positive and productive pursuits, to living a virtuous life.

The true epiphany came to me in 1977. By that time, I was married and the father of two infant children. A journalist from New York by the name of Helen Epstein came to Toronto to interview children of survivors for a cover story in *The New York Times Magazine*.[2] Why Toronto? Helen, whose own parents had endured the concentration camps, heard that an unusually large number of survivors had settled in this city, making it a good place to find subjects. No one had ever touched on this topic before: now that we children had reached adulthood, we were being recognized as people in our own right, influenced, to be sure, by our parents' experiences, yet finally distinct from them, with well-formed thoughts of our own.

The Times story provoked such an overwhelming response that Epstein decided to expand her research into a book, which was published under the title *Children of the Holocaust.*[3] My younger sister Rochelle and I figured quite prominently in it. A major theme of the book was that all of us who had survivor parents grew up thinking we were unique in the world, and it was wonderfully liberating to learn that there were actually many others like us. Though our group is extraordinarily diverse, we share a strong unarticulated sense of kinship grounded in our awareness of things that outsiders could never understand.

Still, I am troubled by the "Second Generation" phenomenon that developed in subsequent years, and I have kept my distance from it. For one thing, I do not want to be pegged narrowly as a child of survivors. I do not deny that I am one, and I am actually proud of it, but this is only a part of who I am, a single component in my broader identity. Furthermore, while it is a sacred obligation to remember, there is no future in dwelling on the past. Throughout our long and troubled history, we Jews have prevailed by choosing and celebrating life, not death.

I am deeply uncomfortable with the notion of people suffering because of the terrible experiences of their parents many years earlier. I am certainly aware that there exist tormented children of survivors, having met a number of them over the years. However, this is simply not *my* story, nor that of the great majority of children of survivors whom I know. It is important to make the point that most of us are not "damaged goods." Not only is it *possible in principle* for survivors to recover from the ravages they endured, to the extent necessary to raise successful and happy children: it has actually been done, many times over. And, it *must be* done. Defeatism and despair only play into the hands of those who would destroy the Jewish people.

Shortly after Epstein's book was published, my wife Renée and I were invited to participate in a young leadership-training program sponsored by the Toronto Jewish Congress. Upon its completion, I was assigned to be a member of the "Holocaust Remembrance Committee." Someone evidently thought this was a natural posting for me, given my background. What I found was a group of elderly survivors totally preoccupied with the tragedy of European Jewry and its commemoration. Many of them had failed to transmit a wholesome Jewish self-image to their own children. This was not at all surprising: I could not imagine any young person wanting to identify with a heritage of victimization and murder, devoid of positive and uplifting content. I found myself choking on the negative energy generated by these morose people, and I could not flee from them quickly enough.

Over the years, my parents were often asked to contribute to "Holocaust Memorial" projects. Their response was invariably unenthusiastic. "Our children and grandchildren are the best memorial to our lost loved ones," they would say. They believed that by raising their children to be proud Jews, they devised a vibrant conduit to the destroyed world of their parents. Instead of commemorating Jewish death, they generously supported projects that celebrated Jewish life and helped secure the Jewish future.

According to Primo Levi, survivors fall into one of two categories: *those who talk and those who do not.*

He is surely describing my parents.

My mother's memories surge out of her in a mighty torrent of words, both spoken and written. This has a powerfully cathartic and healing effect on her. The passionate dignity of her words enables her to impose meaning on that which would otherwise be unbearably meaningless.

My father, on the other hand, never talked about his youth in Hungary or his wartime experiences. It is not just that he refused to talk about the past: if he was in a room with people and the discussion turned to anything remotely connected with the old country or the War, he would try to change the subject. If this did not work, he would find an excuse to leave the room. I have always figured that this was his way of coping with his intensely private personal pain. Who can argue, when the strategy seems to have worked so well for him? This man was able to build a remarkably successful new life by banishing his demons – at least at the conscious level. When he was adrift in the helplessness of sleep, the nightmares held sway.

Like children from other backgrounds, I eventually grew to adulthood and cast off the insecurities of my youth. Seeing what my parents achieved, and appreciating, as I now do, the circumstances of their lives and the struggles they endured, I take pride in the things that made them different. I now understand that my parents were exceptional people, not only because they survived, but also because they preserved their humanity in the face of their enemies' determined efforts to destroy it.

The phases of my parents' life since the War represent a gradual evolution from chaos to order, from meaninglessness to meaning. A significant aspect of the Jewish *spiritual* tragedy in Europe, as opposed to the purely *physical* one, is the inability of many survivors to regain a simple faith in the purposefulness of their lives. My parents' story, for all its heartache and travail, is ultimately a positive one because they succeeded in redeeming their authentic selves. Their steadfastness can serve as an inspiration to those who are tempted to despair of the future as they survey the never-ending depravities and atrocities ravaging the world.

How did they do it? What was the source of their remarkable strength?

I realize that I can never hope to enter my parents' inner sanctum. The knowledge of certain things is destined to remain forever out of bounds to non-survivors, even to the survivors' own children, no matter how deep the love and tight the bonds. Yet, I have, after all, managed to learn a great deal about my parents throughout a lifetime of living close to them. Some things they have taught me, quite deliberately and self-consciously. Other things I have figured out on my own, and my parents would probably find some of these rather surprising, perhaps even upsetting.

Once I began to develop a consciousness and the ability to retain memories, my parents' story began to merge little by little with my own. In time, as I came of age, their story actually became *my* story. With regard to my knowledge of what happened during the first few years in Canada, when I was still an infant, I have no choice but to rely on the accounts of others. In practice, this means that I am heavily dependent on the information that has been transmitted to me by my communicative parent, my dear mother. Her version of the family's early immigrant experience has had a profound impact on me.

In recent years, I have come to realize that matters are not quite so simple. For one thing, my mother's access to information was severely limited by the fact that she was at first a refugee and later an immigrant, isolated by social norms and lack of fluency in English. For another, and perhaps more tellingly, her view of events was strongly influenced by her powerful need to see the good in people as part of her healing process. The contradictions between her charitable view of human nature and the obvious failings of the flesh-and-blood people she encountered in real life were largely lost on me while I was a child. It took me a long time to come to see things in a more nuanced manner.

Once again, Primo Levi, the Torino-born survivor of Auschwitz and master memoirist, provides insight: "Human memory is a marvelous but fallacious instrument. The memories which lie within us are not carved in stone; not only do they tend to become erased as the years go by, but often they change, or even increase by incorporating extraneous features." [4]

For two decades after the end of the Second World War, hardly anything was published regarding the mass murder of the Jews of Europe. The survivors were not yet ready to speak, but neither was the world ready to listen. However, in the years since, we have witnessed an ever-swelling torrent of literature on this subject. There is a growing sense of urgency among the rapidly diminishing aging survivors. They realize that if they do not record their testimony soon, it will be lost forever.

This book is different: it focuses on the post-war process of healing and rehabilitation among survivors, a subject that has received scant attention despite its clear importance. I do not claim that my family's story is typical or representative. I do not even claim that my telling of it necessarily reflects the objective realities in which it is grounded. I must tread very gently in dealing with the view of the past that is my heritage: It has sustained and inspired me, and thus it is sacred to me.

I do believe that my parents bear a stirring message about the astonishing resilience of two particular human beings. I also believe that the success of the few has the power to inspire the many. I have absorbed my parents' story into my very being, and I shall try to transmit it the only way I can, in my own distinct voice. In the process, I hope that I shall be able to provide some answers to the important questions posed above.

I offer the pages that follow in devoted homage to my beloved parents, Judith and Bill Rubinstein.

Judit

Judit lay exhausted in bed, her newborn son snugly bundled beside her. The maternity ward of the Ospedale Maria Vittoria in Torino, Italy was a large room packed with women and babies. The cacophony was deafening. Some of the women were in various stages of labor, shrieking "Mamma mia!" at the top of their lungs. Others had already given birth, and their babies, in bed with them, yelped shrilly, filling in the upper register of the chaotic chorus. It was hardly a tranquil place to recuperate, but Judit was so thrilled about the wondrous event she had just experienced that she barely noticed the din. She could not possibly have imagined, as a prisoner in Auschwitz, that a mere three years later she would be privileged to bring a Jewish child into the world, without fear for his safety.

It was early spring in northern Italy. The windows in the maternity ward had been flung wide open, and the aroma of blooming roses wafted in from the hospital's garden. Spring. Rebirth. Judit was seized by a sense of promise for the future. The hospital staff had already affectionately labeled her son "*piccolo polacchino*," little Pole. They made the rather reasonable assumption that any foreigner to be found in Torino those days was of Polish origin. Despite the fact that she was obviously not Italian, the staff treated Judit no differently than the others. This in itself was astonishing for someone who had not long before been harshly mistreated simply because she was Jewish. It seemed there were still good-hearted people left in the world. Perhaps her despair had been premature: perhaps there was hope for mankind after all.

13

Yet, as she glanced around the room on that glorious spring morning, Judit was reminded of her desperate loneliness. She knew not a soul in the hospital. Her son had been born on a Friday afternoon, shortly before the onset of the Sabbath. Her husband, Béla, had to leave the hospital while she was still in labor, in order to make it back to Grugliasco before nightfall. He did this out of respect for the Sabbath, on which he was not permitted to travel. He also did it out of respect for the curfew requiring all refugees to be inside the camp's walls by eight o'clock every night. That entire day, neither Béla nor anyone else who would be interested knew for certain that Judit had given birth. She yearned to share her joy with those she loved, and she was deeply saddened by the fact that she could not do so. At this special moment, when she became for the first time a giver of life, Judit ached with longing for her own mother.

Every child is indebted to her parents for the gift of life.
Since the War, Judit has been possessed of a strong conviction that she received life from her own mother not once, but twice. Over the years since their tragic parting, she has been burdened with regret that she never had the opportunity to thank her mother for this extraordinary gift.

When the Germans came to deport the Jews of Szerencs, Hungary in 1944, they herded Judit, together with her parents and the two youngest of her three brothers, Shimon and Eliezer, into a tightly packed cattle-car. The people on the train were told that they were being taken to Germany to work in factories in support of the war effort. For several days, they traveled in the most degrading conditions, lacking sanitary facilities, water, or food. Finally, they arrived, not in Germany but in Oswiecim, a Polish town of which none of them had ever heard. It was May 20, a bright, sunny day. The train unloaded its exhausted human cargo, along with quite a number of dead bodies, as men in SS uniforms looked on, guns at the ready. Other men in striped pajamas pulled people off the train. At the entrance to the camp was a high iron gate bearing the slogan *"ARBEIT MACHT FREI"* (Work makes you free). On one platform, musicians dressed in ubiquitous striped pajamas welcomed the new arrivals with classical music.

Before the family left the train, Judit's father blessed her in accordance with the ancient tradition. He urged her to eat whatever food the Germans gave her, without regard for the Jewish dietary laws that he had raised her to respect. He also advised her always to be the first to volunteer for work. He understood that these two things, combined with a large measure of good luck, could save her life. Eliahu Schwarcz had a better grasp of reality than most of the Jews who arrived at Oswiecim that day.

A few minutes later, he disappeared with Shimon. Judit was never to see either of them again.

She was standing huddled with her mother and her little brother Eliezer, when along came a high-ranking SS officer who she later learned was the infamous Dr. Josef Mengele. He started the "selection" among the women, sending the older-looking women and the mothers with children to one side, and sending the young and healthy-looking girls and women to the other side, filed five in a row.

What her mother did next will remain forever seared into Judit's memory.

In front of them were standing four tall, good-looking girls in their late teens whom they knew from the ghetto, holding the hands of their three little nieces and a nephew. Her mother pulled these children to her side, and pushed Judit to be the fifth in a row with the four girls. "I will take care of the children," she told them, "and you will take care of Judit." Within a minute, her mother disappeared with the four children. That was the last time Judit ever saw her.

Over the years, Judit has often wondered how her mother could possibly have known that she would save her daughter by separating her from the children and herself. Maternal instinct perhaps, sharpened by the extremity of the situation? To this day, while enduring sleepless nights, she thinks of the agony this special woman must have suffered before she perished in the gas chamber with the children and the countless other martyrs. The pain of losing her so young and in such a terrible way has accompanied Judit throughout her life.[1]

As she lay in bed with her baby son in the room full of strange women, Judit's thoughts drifted past the hellish experience of being torn forever from her own mother. Throughout the time she was imprisoned in Auschwitz and up until her liberation, she had to focus single-mindedly on the daily challenge of staying alive. She was privileged to witness astounding acts of heroism in the camp, such as the October 1944 uprising by several hundred male prisoners, who succeeded in blowing up one of the crematoria and a gas chamber. They used explosives smuggled into the camp by Jewish women working in a nearby ammunition plant. The enraged Germans shot the rebels and hanged the explosives smugglers in a public spectacle. Although Judit deeply admired her fellow prisoners' valiant conduct, she was determined to honor her father's plea that she do her best to survive. But with large numbers of ordinary, unheroic people dropping like flies all around her every day, it was increasingly difficult to preserve a sense of her worth as a human being.

Her thoughts meandered on to the period following the end of the War, when she was just starting the slow, difficult process of reclaiming her humanity.

The group of ten ragged and emaciated young women was shuffling along in the ditch by the side of the road leading into Schwerin, Germany. Along with hundreds of other inmates, they had been marched out of Auschwitz many days earlier by their German captors, ahead of the Red Army advancing into Poland from the east. Judit's wise and resourceful older cousin, Regina Hofstadter, was acknowledged as the group's leader. At that moment, it was impossible to appreciate the full significance of what was happening. Tank after tank rumbled past on the road, each one flying the proud flag of the United States of America. The Nazis guarding them on the march had disappeared so quietly, so meekly into the fields alongside, that the young women were startled when they realized their tormentors were gone.

They had grown accustomed to having their every move scrutinized, under the constant threat of beatings and shootings. Now, all of a sudden, they were invisible: no one took the least notice of them, neither the American soldiers focused on their mission nor the terrified German civilians who wished *they* could be invisible. The young women moved about furtively, not knowing what to do. It certainly appeared that they were now free of the Germans, but they had been conditioned by recent experience to be extremely cautious and suspicious. They were not sure what to make of the Americans, who they wanted to believe were friendly, but who were too preoccupied with pacifying the region to make their intentions clear. Finally, the young women came across an abandoned, badly damaged office building. They settled into a room on the first floor with the scraps of food they had managed to scavenge along the way.

Judit will always remember the dramatic circumstances of her first encounter with the American soldiers: for her, this was the demarcation line between her old, shattered world and the new one, so burdened by uncertainty yet filled with hope.

In the concentration camps, in quiet defiance of the Nazis, many Jewish inmates had maintained their spirits and preserved their sense of self by keeping track of the Sabbath and the Jewish holidays. The girls who had been huddling in the abandoned office building for two weeks knew that the night of May 17, 1945 was the beginning of *Shavuos*, the holiday commemorating God's giving of the Torah to the Jewish people at Mount Sinai. Somehow, they were able to find two candles. With nightfall, they lit them on the windowsill in honor of the holiday and recited the traditional blessing. There was no electrical power, so the candles provided the only illumination.

Soon there was a furious rapping on the door. Two soldiers burst in. One of them screamed in German: "Don't you know there is a curfew in effect? Why do you have lights in the window?"

Regina stepped forward and responded calmly in her impeccable Pressburger High German: "We are ten Jewish women who have survived the Auschwitz concentration camp. Now that we are finally free of the Nazis, we expect to be able to celebrate our holiday, which starts tonight, in peace."

The American soldiers froze. Overwhelmed with emotion, they began to weep, for lo and behold, they were also Jewish. Tears running down their faces, they hugged and kissed each of the girls in turn. They had been given to believe that not a single Jew survived Auschwitz. The next morning, Captain Sol Kopel of Houston and Sergeant Herbert Saafeld of the Bronx returned with the company medic and a military truck. They drove the girls to a villa on the outskirts of town belonging to an elderly German couple, and settled them into the unimaginably luxurious comfort of the second floor. They watched over their charges lovingly, speaking with them in Yiddish and nursing them back to health by patiently feeding them nourishing food. Captain Kopel, a middle-aged gentleman with a wife and four children back home, grew particularly fond of Judit. He offered to adopt her, in order to facilitate her immigration to the United States. Deeply touched by this generous gesture, she thanked him and explained that she was anxious to go home to Hungary and rejoin her own family. The Jewish officer from distant America knew that it was unlikely she would find anyone, but he did not have the heart to shatter her illusions.

Every day, soldiers from the company came to visit, bearing gifts of cigarettes and chocolate. (Cigarettes? Could you eat them? And chocolate? Who had been audacious enough to even *dream* of chocolate in Auschwitz?) One soldier brought a battered old gramophone and a scratchy recording of Gounod's *Ave Maria.* The girls played it over and over again, quite oblivious to its Roman Catholic liturgical origin. To this day, *Ave Maria* is one of my mother's favorite pieces of music.

Another G.I. found an antiquated but still operable sewing machine. He presented it to Judit, the seamstress in the group. Someone else brought sets of navy-blue-and-white-checked bed sheets from the abandoned local Nazi headquarters. Judit sewed an identical navy-blue-and-white-checked dress, with a wide skirt, puffy sleeves, and a little white collar, for each of the ten girls. They did look a bit odd when they all got together, but the new clothes were a huge improvement over the rags they had worn from Auschwitz. Little by little, they were starting to feel like human beings again.

Judit knew that these Americans must have been battle-hardened warriors trained to kill without hesitation or remorse. Yet, she was struck by the fact that they were also warm, compassionate human beings, capable of bestowing kindness on total strangers. It was a good thing for her to be reminded just then that people could be *that* way as well. The range of possibilities arrayed before her was suddenly much broader than it had been only a short time earlier.

For a genuinely good-hearted person like Judit, it had been a great shock to realize that there were people in the world who hated her with a murderous passion, not because of anything she had done to them, but simply because of her Jewish ancestry. Long before Auschwitz, she had been deeply disturbed to learn that expressions of kindness, far from inspiring reciprocal behavior, sometimes provoked the exact opposite.

When Judit was growing up, there lived in her town of Szerencs a destitute and sad-eyed woman whom everyone called Juli Néni (Auntie Juli). She had three illegitimate children, two girls and a boy named Gyula. Taking pity on her, Judit's mother and other housewives in the Jewish community gave Juli Néni work as a washerwoman. Gyula accompanied

18

his mother when she went to the Jewish homes to do the laundry. A strapping, restless lad, he was always hungry. Judit's mother would give him a large bowl of steaming cabbage soup which he devoured with gusto. She also gave him the clothing that her oldest son, Yitzchak, had outgrown.

When the fascist Arrow Cross movement established a branch in Szerencs, Gyula joined with great enthusiasm. By now grown tall and strong, he finally found a place where he could hold his head high. He rose rapidly through the ranks to become the local leader of the Arrow Cross. Gyula achieved notoriety in the Jewish community by strutting about with his gang of brutes, viciously tormenting the very people who had once been so kind to him and to his mother. It seems this was his way of coping with the humiliation and frustration of his impoverished childhood. It was also a classic manifestation of the paradoxical phenomenon known as anti-Semitism.

The Jews of Szerencs, like Jews all over German-occupied Europe, were dumbfounded by the murderous onslaught that was soon unleashed against them. They could not understand why they were hated with such burning intensity. Certainly, individual Jews had their faults, as did all mere mortals. But the great majority were law-abiding citizens who contributed at least their fair share to society and, often, far more. Surely, they were not so bad that they deserved to be annihilated. So detached from reality were most of the Jews of Szerencs that they obediently got on the trains, believing the soldiers' stories about going to work in factories to assist the German war effort. They were quite incapable of imagining the terrible fate awaiting them.

After her liberation, Judit returned to Szerencs, hoping that her loved ones had somehow survived. Strangers were now living in her home, and they were certainly not pleased to see one of the Jews returning to reclaim, as they imagined, her family's property. She was heartened by the arrival several days later of her brother Yitzchak. He had been separated from the rest of the family and placed on a different train heading to Auschwitz. Refusing to submit passively to fate like the others, Yitzchak had managed to pry open the door of the cattle-car and roll out into the nocturnal darkness of the Hungarian countryside. The resourceful young man found his way to Budapest, where he was sheltered and saved by the Swedish hero, Raoul Wallenberg.

As the days and weeks passed without any trace of her beloved parents and younger brothers, Judit began to despair. Then, one day, as she was walking down the main street, she spotted her mother some distance ahead. She would have recognized that gray dress anywhere, as she had sewn it with her own hands not long before the Jews of Szerencs were deported. In a frenzy of joy, she started running forward, screaming "Mother, mother!"

The startled woman turned around. It was not her mother, but one of the old Hungarian neighbors. She had obviously helped herself to Rozsa Schwarcz's wardrobe, in the expectation that neither she nor any of the other Jews of Szerencs would ever return. Her expression of surprise quickly turned to one of contemptuous hatred, as if to say, "What a shame they missed one of you!" Crying hysterically, Judit turned and ran away. She found Yitzchak and easily persuaded him that there was nothing left for them in the town that had once been their home. As they headed for the train station, Judit vowed to herself that she would never again set foot in that accursed place.

If Judit remembered her own mother as the two-fold giver of life, she remembered her father as the guide and mentor who sustained her spirit long after he was so cruelly torn away from her. Eliahu Schwarcz was tall and dignified, patient and soft-spoken, kind-hearted and attentive, a lover of books and ideas. Judit cherished every moment she was able to spend with him.

In Auschwitz, she had received reports, right down to the waning days of the War when the Germans marched her to Schwerin, that her father was still alive in the camp. For a long time after she finally accepted the bitter reality that her mother and younger brothers would never come back, she continued to harbor the desperate hope that her father had been "liberated" by the Russians and shipped off to Siberia, like so many others. As the years passed beyond any reasonable limit, the hope gradually faded away.

Because of the circumstances at the time, Judit was unable to salvage a single photograph or other tangible memento of her parents and brothers. Several years ago, she was reading a book chronicling the murder of the Jews of Hungary.[2] When she got to the photograph section toward the end of the book, she froze. There, in a photograph captioned "Work unit in Sarospatak, October 1940", was her father, tall and dignified, mustachioed and wearing an overcoat and fedora. He was standing in a row of Jewish men who had been conscripted into forced labor, facing two smirking Hungarian soldiers. The facts fitted her recollection that her father had been taken to a *munkatabor*, a forced labor camp in Sarospatak, in October 1940. As he was deemed too old to be of any value to the Fatherland, he was sent home shortly afterwards, to be transported to Auschwitz together with his family in 1944.

Judit had the picture enlarged and framed, and she displays it prominently in her home. Was the man in the picture really her father? There is probably no way of telling, but in truth, it does not matter. This tangible connection to the past gives her solace.

Eliahu Schwarcz did not like what he saw happening in Hungary. Laws limiting Jews' basic rights had already been passed in 1920, and in subsequent years, Jews were gradually deprived of their possessions, freedom, and dignity. The government of Regent Horthy had enacted the First and Second Jewish Laws of 1938 and 1939, in which Hungarian Jews were declared second-class citizens.

Most Jews were very slow to read the writing on the wall. They were, after all, ardent patriots who had consistently demonstrated unfailing devotion to their country. However, in their eagerness to be loved and accepted in return, their judgment was badly clouded, and they did not grasp the meaning of the ominous events unfolding before their eyes.

One of the few whose vision remained clear was Eliahu Schwarcz's father-in-law, Aryeh Leib Hofstadter. Every day, he would read the newspaper of the Arrow Cross. Whenever a grandchild expressed astonishment that he would expose himself to such scurrilous anti-Semitic drivel, he responded in the Galician Yiddish of his youth: "*Mein kind, zai zogn dem emes.*" (My child, they are telling the truth.) He did not mean, of course, that the content of the newspaper was factually correct. He was saying that anyone who wanted to glimpse the future of the Jews in Hungary was better served by reading the fascist press than by reading the head-in-the-sand Jewish papers.

Oblivious as most Hungarian Jews were to what was happening to their brethren in neighboring countries, there were plenty of warning signs available to those who cared to see them. Shortly after the German invasion of Poland at the start of the War, the Schwarcz children began, at their father's initiative, to put together small packages of basic foodstuffs, which were mailed to Jewish families in Poland assumed to be in need of assistance. After a while, the packages started coming back. "Return to sender," they were marked. "Addressee has moved, no forwarding address provided."

Eliahu Schwarcz did not hesitate to draw the obvious conclusion, even if many others resisted doing so. He also agreed with his hardheaded father-in-law's highly unpopular assessment of the situation. This led him to what was in his circle the radical step of becoming a Zionist. The *Hitkozseg*, the official Jewish community organization in Szerencs, was staunchly anti-Zionist, reflecting the sentiments of the great majority of European Jews at the time. They simply could not countenance the terrible possibility that their love of country might not be reciprocated. Eliahu Schwarcz, for his part, saw no hope for the Jews in Hungary, and he was determined to take his family to *Eretz Yisrael*, the Land of Israel, the historic homeland of the Jewish people.

As secretary of the Szerencs *Hitkozseg*, he was often called upon to help members of the community. An early case was the Merzel family, who had emigrated from Poland several years earlier and did not yet hold Hungarian citizenship. The government ordered the family deported back to German-occupied Poland, where they faced a most uncertain future. Eliahu Schwarcz traveled to Budapest and demanded that the Hungarian Zionist Organization get these imperiled Jews to *Eretz Yisrael*. Thanks to his efforts, the Merzel family survived the War.

Many others followed. When his family, their anxiety growing by the day, asked their patriarch how he could help other people get out of Hungary while his own kin remained behind, his response was that the captain is always the last to leave a sinking ship. By the time he finally got around to his own family, it was too late: the borders were sealed, and no Jew was permitted to leave the country. In an act as tragically ineffectual as it was defiant, Eliahu Schwarcz fired off an urgent telegram to Budapest, to the by then banned Zionist Organization, demanding that each and every person in his family be registered as a card-carrying member.

A short time later, they were all deported to Auschwitz.

My mother stayed at the Ospedale Maria Vittoria for two weeks, as was then customary for women who had given birth. Early in the morning of the eighth day, which was a Friday, I was circumcised, and thereby inducted formally into the Jewish people. Professor Doctor Levi, a local physician and member of the Torino Jewish community, performed the circumcision. The entire family came in from Grugliasco to celebrate the joyous occasion. For survivors in those days, the birth of every Jewish child was an event of cosmic significance, a victory over the evil ones who sought to contrive a world devoid of Jewish children. One of the family members, Béla Zimmerman, was given the honor of removing me from my blanket in preparation for the ceremony. Béla remarked on the unusual length of my legs, and predicted that I would grow to be very tall. My parents named me Eliahu Mordechai, after my two deceased grandfathers. I was to be their memorial candle.

Soon after the circumcision, my proud parents went into town to register the birth. The clerk at the Torino City Hall started asking questions and writing their responses onto the birth certificate: Date of birth? *March 5, 1948.* Names of parents? *Béla and Judit Rubinstein.* Nationality of parents? *Stateless.* Name of child? *Eliahu Mordechai.* The clerk reacted to this last response with a puzzled glance. "*Scuzate.* Could you repeat that, please?" *Eliahu Mordechai:* two Hebrew names. "I am truly sorry, but neither of those is on the approved list of male Christian names. Here is the list. You can pick any name you like, as long as it is on the list." My parents were deeply disappointed. They had their hearts set on naming their firstborn after their deceased fathers, in accordance with Jewish tradition. But what could they do? My birth had to be registered. They glanced down the list and saw that "Roberto" was on it. My father's brother Dezso and his wife Vera had very much wanted to give this name to their child born two months earlier, but alas, she was a girl who became known as Anna. So, Roberto it would be. But my parents were determined that, whatever was written on the birth certificate, my real name, the name I was given at my circumcision ceremony and which would forever define me, would be Eliahu Mordechai.

Béla

Since childhood, I have struggled to understand my father. I am not referring to the man of the recent past, for he is someone whom I came to know very well. The man of the distant past is another matter altogether. As my father hardly ever spoke about the earlier part of his life, almost everything of the little I do know concerning this period has come to me from indirect sources.

Reflecting back on the years I was privileged to know him, two rare instances of my father opening up about his past stand out in my memory.

The first related to his unusually youthful appearance, a consequence of his rosy-cheeked, virtually wrinkle-free complexion. I once mentioned this to him, and was quite surprised by his explanation. In April of 1943, he was in a *munkatabor,* a forced labor camp on the outskirts of Budapest, working in a munitions factory. One day, the air-raid siren sounded, signaling an imminent attack by enemy aircraft. Before anyone could take shelter, a large bomb came crashing through the roof. It ignited the phosphorous supply and sent a searing flash of fire through the plant. My father lost consciousness and fell to the floor. He was taken to a hospital in Budapest, where he convalesced for many months. The explosion of the bomb at close quarters had punctured his eardrums, while the phosphoric blaze had burned off all his hair and turned the skin of his face totally black. This skin eventually peeled off, exposing a baby-pink new epidermis. Thus, my father explained his youthful-looking face.

It was as if, in narrowly cheating death, my father had one part of his physicality reborn. An eerie foreshadowing, perhaps, of the spiritual renaissance he was to undergo after the War.

The second uncommon glimpse into my father's past was provided several years ago. We had gone to the neighborhood synagogue to hear a respected Talmudic scholar speak about "The Meaning of the Holocaust." The learned rabbi expounded upon the classical Jewish idea that when God permits calamity to befall the Children of Israel, it is because they have been sinful. In his view, the Jews of Europe must have angered God very badly, and the murder of six million of them was the catastrophic consequence. The rabbi suggested that perhaps these people had not been sufficiently scrupulous in their performance of the commandments.

Visibly agitated, my father rose from his seat and left the room. For someone who was generally a paragon of courtesy, such an act was quite out of character. He explained to me afterwards that he had reacted sharply to the suggestion that the murdered members of his family were responsible for their fate rather than the Nazi murderers. He found this notion obscene. As my father saw it, someone like the guest speaker was only able to express such a warped view of things because he had the good fortune to survive the War in the safety of his American home. Any Jew who had lived through the hell of wartime Europe knew better.

Such fragments – an anecdote here, a sharp reaction there – are all my father ever conveyed to me directly regarding his past and how he felt about it. It fell to my mother to provide me with a key piece of information about my father, which radically transformed my understanding of him.

Shortly after I turned sixteen, my mother took me aside and told me she had something important to tell me. It was very difficult for her to talk about it, but she wanted me to hear it from her before I heard it from some stranger. I didn't know what to think. *Perhaps she was going to tell me that I had been adopted?* No, that was not it. She revealed that my father had previously been married with two young sons. He and his family lived happily in Szentistvan, the village of his birth. During the War, he was drafted into forced labor by the Hungarian government, along with many other able-bodied Jewish men. He was working in a munitions factory when the Americans dropped a bomb on the building, and he was gravely wounded. While he was recuperating in a hospital in Budapest, drifting deliriously in and out of consciousness, his wife and children were deported to Auschwitz, never to return. He was completely unaware of what had happened to them until he was able to go home at war's end. He never fully recovered from the terrible tragedy of losing his family. What made the tragedy painful beyond bearing was his sense of failure as a husband and father, and his irrational feelings of guilt at not being present to protect his loved ones when they desperately needed him.

I was in shock. I ran to my room, closed the door, and started crying uncontrollably. Later I would wonder: *What was it that upset me so? Was it grief over the murder of my stepbrothers and their mother? Was it a son's shared experience of his father's pain? Or, was it perhaps the realization by a sensitive young man that his own father was in some ways a stranger to him?*

Béla Rubinstein was born in 1908 in the remote agricultural village of Szentistvan, Hungary. Whatever fresh winds may have been blowing in larger, more important places, the world he entered was of an earlier and simpler time. The local peasants ploughed their fields with the help of horses, just as their wild Magyar ancestors had done after storming into Europe from the steppes of central Asia. Horses, drawing wooden carts, also provided transportation along the rutted, muddy road leading through the village. The nearest train station was kilometers away, but most residents of Szentistvan never had occasion to go there; rarely did people venture further afield than the villages neighboring their own. They lived their lives blissfully unaware of novelties in the larger world beyond such as electrical power, indoor plumbing, automobiles, telephones, and radio.

The people of Szentistvan were simple farming folk who had always enjoyed cordial relations with the few Jewish families living in their midst. In such a small place, people could hardly help being well integrated with one another. The Jews owned the few businesses in the village, and by all accounts, they treated both employees and customers fairly. All of the children attended the same tiny public school, and the same teacher taught them all. In the afternoons, they played together in the fields surrounding the village.

Even if my father had been more forthcoming about the past, we would still know almost nothing about the genealogy and the history of his family. One of the few things we do know is that my grandfather, Mordechai Rubinstein, was a self-made man. Both of his parents had died in unknown circumstances when he was very young, and by default, the burden of raising his two younger sisters fell on his shoulders. So seriously did he take this responsibility that well after he himself had come of age, he did not go looking for a wife of his own until he succeeded in finding suitable young men for his sisters to marry. Mordechai never had the opportunity to be a child – to play, to be mischievous. From early on, he had to concentrate on making a living. He eventually became a dealer in animal pelts, and his natural aptitude for business enabled him to become quite prosperous, at least by the standards of a remote and unpretentious Hungarian peasant village.

At the appropriate time, Mordechai married Rivka, a lovely woman who was, like him, a genealogical cipher, and she brought six children into the world. Of these children, we know nothing except that they perished one after the other in the course of an unspecified plague, perhaps typhus. My stoical grandmother overcame her grief and started a second family, bearing another six children. The Rubinsteins had a housekeeper, a widow named Tera Néni, who lived in the family home with her own children. Her son Pista was a contemporary of Béla and his brother Dezso, the two youngest of the Rubinstein children. The three of them grew up together as the best of friends.

Yet, cordial as the relations between Jews and Christians were in such a tiny place, everyone in the village was aware of the lines that could never be crossed. In a conservative rural community, religion served as an effective barrier to social interaction.

On the Sabbath and Jewish holidays, the Jews kept completely to themselves, praying and enjoying long, festive meals. Their strict dietary laws ensured that they never sat down to a meal with the gentile neighbors. And when the *melamed* (traditional teacher) came to Szentistvan every week to teach the Jewish children the basics of their heritage, they were not available to play with their friends. The peasants, for their part, would go to the little Roman Catholic Church in the village on Sundays and holy days. There, they would hear from the priest how the Jews were responsible for the crucifixion of the Lord, and how they are forever accursed for having rejected him. The more reflective among the congregants must have been puzzled about the disjunction between the sinister

Jews described by the priest and the good Jews living in their midst. But things were as they were, as they had always been. Everyone in Szentistvan knew his place in the divinely ordained scheme of things.

Their personal experience certainly gave the people of Szentistvan no reason to bear ill will toward their Jewish neighbors. Indeed, there was considerable evidence of genuine affection and appreciation. However, in the dark days of 1944 when the Germans came to take the Jews away, there were no heroes to be found. None of the villagers risked their own safety or that of their families to help the neighbors who had been so good to them.

When the War finally ended, Béla went home to Szentistvan, hoping to find his family. He had no difficulty reclaiming his property: no one would have dreamt of moving into the Rubinstein home, as happened so commonly in other places. Yet, it seemed the villagers had been powerless to prevent the looting of the house's contents.

Upon his return, however, Béla found not his family, but the Soviet occupation forces. The Russians assumed he was a Hungarian soldier, and treated him harshly. When the local commandant interrogated him, Béla was able to explain through the interpreter that he was actually a Jew who had been drafted into forced labor by the Hungarian army. In a curious twist, the commandant turned out to be Jewish himself, but this did not make him any friendlier. He wanted to know why Béla had not run away and joined the partisans, or resisted the Germans in some other manner. Béla feared the worst: he was sure he would be sent to Siberia, but to his astonishment, the commandant let him go.

As the occupying power, the Soviets were responsible for feeding the local population. There was plenty of wheat growing in the fields, but there was no functioning mill in which to grind it into flour. The Rubinstein flourmill had been sitting idle during the time the men were in forced labor. The commandant summoned Béla and ordered him to put it back into operation. This was not a simple matter, as someone had looted key components of the mill. In addition, Béla's expertise had always been on the administrative side. It was his brother Dezso, present whereabouts unknown, who had been the technical expert responsible for the actual operation of the equipment. The commandant promised to get Béla whatever supplies he needed. With Pista's help, he eventually succeeded in reactivating the flourmill.

Tera Néni moved back into the Rubinstein home, and once again took charge of running a proper Jewish household. The rooms were spruced up and the pantry was stocked with provisions. Day after day, Béla waited for his family to appear at the door. After a few months, the terrible realization finally sank in: his wife and two young sons must have been killed at Auschwitz. Such was the tragic fate of the aged, the infirm, the children, and most of the women in his extended family, as well as almost all the other Jews of the village who had been deported while the able-bodied men were away in the forced labor camps. In time, Bandi, the son of Béla's eldest brother Isidor, straggled back to Szentistvan. So did Dezso, suffering from a badly crushed left leg; but his wife Vera, who had been in her seventh month of pregnancy when she was deported, never returned.

When Passover came around, Béla invited the tiny group of Jews who had made it back home to a *Seder*, to create a semblance of normality and to enable them to take comfort in one another's company. Tera Néni lovingly cooked all the traditional dishes, using the recipes she had learned from Rivka, the matriarch of the Rubinstein family. Béla also invited a Russian doctor, a Yiddish-speaking Jew who was working at the local hospital. Everyone at the table was curious to know why the Soviets were not taking revenge on their German prisoners for all the dreadful things they had done during the War. The doctor turned to Béla and said, "You Jewish businessmen! You will never be good Communists. Those Nazis, though, one day they will be excellent Communists."

With the arrival in Szentistvan of the Red Army, the once-menacing Arrow Cross militiamen vanished. The Hungarian Communists soon took their place, looking for competent people to form a local organization. Being far more pragmatic than the Russian Jewish doctor, they targeted Béla Rubinstein, one of the very few individuals left in the peasant backwater who was literate and possessed managerial skills. He was notified that, henceforth, he would serve as the secretary of the Szentistvan branch of the Hungarian Communist Party. He knew, of course, that it would be imprudent to decline. He was too depressed about the loss of his loved ones to be amused by the irony of the situation. Imagine, an incorrigible capitalist like him being appointed a servant of the Proletariat!

A Match Made in Mezokovesd

When they realized that their parents and brothers would never return, Judit and Yitzchak Schwarcz turned their backs on Szerencs. There could be no future for them in the town that had once been their home. They took the train to Budapest where, they had heard, a central registry of concentration camp survivors was being compiled. Struggling through the frenzied mob at the registry office, they learned that two of their uncles were alive and had returned home. They left Budapest, first traveling to Mezocsat to stay for a while with their paternal uncle, Yanki Schwarcz, who had nearly died of typhus. While there, they wrote a letter to Wili Hofstadter, their mother's brother, inquiring about his welfare.

Wili Bacsi ("Uncle Willy" in Hungarian) had survived Mauthausen along with his sons Imi and Sanyi, but his wife, Matild Néni ("Aunt Matilda"), had perished in the gas chambers. Judit and Yitzchak soon learned that the brutal abuse he suffered in the camp had left their uncle very ill, both physically and emotionally. When Wili Bacsi pleaded with Judit to come stay with him in his hometown of Mezokovesd, she agreed. Patiently, lovingly, she nursed her uncle back to health as if she were attending to one of her own parents. Wili Bacsi, for his part, was determined to honor his sister's memory by finding a suitable husband for his orphaned niece.

Despite her rough treatment at the hands of the Nazis only a short while before, Judit was, at the age of twenty-four, a very attractive young woman. In normal times, it would not have been difficult finding her a suitable mate. Unfortunately, the times were anything but normal. A great many lives had been ripped apart, and there was among the survivors a sense of

30

desperation about the need to rebuild Jewish families. This led to a dropping of conventional inhibitions and demonstrations of appallingly poor judgment from people who might have been expected to know better.

Wili Bacsi did not take long to arrive at a decision: his niece would marry a certain first cousin who, like her, was a war orphan. The young man readily agreed, and Wili Bacsi set about preparing for the wedding. Judit was stunned. She and her cousin had nothing in common, and she recoiled at the idea of marrying so close a relative. Most importantly, he wanted to continue living in Hungary as if nothing had happened, while Judit was determined to go with Yitzchak to *Eretz Yisrael*. When she tried to explain her feelings to her uncle, he became quite annoyed with her. The only person who could console and encourage her was her cousin, Sanyi. He urged her to follow her heart and not allow his father to pressure her into something she would later regret.

No sooner had Judit recovered from this fiasco than another one of her uncles showed up in Mezokovesd. This gentleman had been married to a maternal aunt who did not return from Auschwitz. He came right to the point: *Here they were, two people in need of spouses, so why not marry one another?* Judit explained, as gently as she could, that she was unable to marry a man who was the same age as her father. The uncle never spoke to her again.

Other prospective matches materialized, one more preposterous than the next. Judit began to wonder: *Where were all the good men? Had every last one been killed by the Nazis?*

Annoyed as he was with his stubborn niece, Wili Bacsi could not rest until he completed his mission. He looked around, and fixed his sights on Béla Rubinstein. Wili Bacsi knew the Rubinstein family well. They lived only seven kilometers away in Szentistvan. His own father, Aryeh Leib, had been the best friend of Béla's father, Mordechai, his partner in the "*mitzvah* business." Together, they sought out people in the community who were in need of financial assistance, and granted them loans that were seldom repaid. Judit had heard about the Rubinsteins from Magdi Schwarcz, a daughter of Béla's older sister Leah, whom she had come to know very well in Auschwitz. From Magdi, she already knew that the Rubinsteins were a warm and closely-knit family, just the kind of family she craved after the tragic loss of her own.

Béla had received word through his political connections that the new Communist government in Hungary was planning to nationalize all privately held businesses and to seal the borders. Up until then, he had consoled himself with the knowledge that while he had lost his wife and children, at least he still had his flourmill and his house. If the authorities were now going to take those things away from him, he really had no reason to stay in Hungary. He was determined to get out while there was still a chance, and a group of family members with the same intention coalesced around him.

Béla was not thinking at that moment of remarrying. He was still grieving the loss of his beloved Ibolya. Besides, the urgent priority just then was to get out of Hungary. There would be plenty of time later on for rebuilding his family.

Béla's brother-in-law, Miklos Fogel, learned of his plans. He urged Béla and Dezso to find themselves local women before they left Hungary, women who spoke their language and shared their values. They would have enough strange and unfamiliar things to adjust to, and taking along a little home-style stability would be beneficial to them. Miklos succeeded in bringing the brothers around to his view of things.

Judit and Béla met and got along well. Béla was twelve years her senior, but after her recent calamitous experience, this seemed to Judit an inconsequential difference. They decided to marry at the first opportunity. There was, however, a complication. Although Ibolya was presumed to have been killed in Auschwitz, there were no surviving eyewitnesses to her death. Under Jewish law, Béla needed a special rabbinic dispensation to remarry. Judit agreed to leave Hungary with him on the understanding that their destination was *Eretz Yisrael*. The wedding would have to wait for a more settled time.

Dezso met a vivacious young woman from Mezokovesd whose name, coincidentally, was Vera. They hit it off nicely and decided to marry. At the same time, Sanyi courted Kicsi, Magdi Schwarcz's youngest sister. Magdi had just married Béla Zimmerman, and the third sister, Borika, had just married her cousin Jeno Schwarcz. This group, along with the oldest Rubinstein brother, Armin, came together as a band of aspiring fugitives. Everyone agreed that the main concern was to get out of the country as quickly as possible.

On the first of April 1946, in the dead of night, the members of the group peered out of the train window at the receding lights of the border crossing. They had just passed from Hungary into Yugoslavia. Seized by a dizzying mix of anticipation and dread, they looked at one another without uttering a word. The die was cast: they knew they had crossed their Rubicon. The train rolled along through the Yugoslav countryside.

Judit was tired of the wandering. It was just a year since the retreating Germans had forced her to walk all the way from Auschwitz into Germany, to Ravensbruck, then Malchow, and finally, to Schwerin. How elated she had been to see the American soldiers, her liberators. Much as she appreciated her newfound freedom, what she appreciated most just then was that she could finally stop wandering.

So here she was, on the move again. Although she dreamed of reaching *Eretz Yisrael*, in truth, she had no idea where she would end up. At least this time she was wandering of her own volition, with her husband-to-be and the rest of her new family-in-the-making.

The train lurched to a stop in the Zagreb station. While the refugees had crossed safely from Hungary into Yugoslavia, they could not yet let down their guard. Both countries were occupied by the Soviet Union, and the travelers were afraid of being caught and punished for having left Hungary illegally. They had paid someone to concoct false papers identifying them as Palestinian Jews trapped in Europe during the War who were now trying to get back home. They dared not speak Hungarian to one another, and they were in constant fear of being stopped and interrogated.

Their luck ran out in Zagreb, as the local police boarded the train, arrested them, and deposited them in prison. What a horrible feeling, to have been liberated finally from the Nazi tyranny, only to be prisoners once again. Fortunately, they soon learned, they were in a country where a little money could go a long way. After Armin bribed the police chief, they were able to leave Yugoslavia and cross the border into Italy.

In Italy, they joined a motley band of about one hundred fifty Jewish refugees from all over Europe. The acknowledged leader was a nineteen-year-old from Poland by the name of Moshe, a veteran of several concentration camps and the sole survivor of his family. Moshe was the exact opposite of his biblical namesake, supremely self-confident and possessed of a silver tongue, but lacking in good judgment and strategic skills. Moshe's bluff and bluster, and, no doubt, an abundance of sheer good luck, saved his charges from a series of catastrophes in the course of their wanderings.

It was most appropriate that the leader of such a group be a mere child thrust into adulthood: Moshe's story was really everyone's story. Their elders had been torn roughly from them, depriving them of the deep wisdom that comes only from years of experience.

The ragtag throng eventually found its way to the Jewish community center in the open city of Trieste. Moshe had heard from someone that this was where Jewish refugees who happened to be in northern Italy were supposed to meet. By the time the group got there, the building was already packed with earlier arrivals. The residents of the neighborhood could not but notice the tumultuous and highly suspicious mob gathering in the usually tranquil building. They called the police who, having no idea what to do, surrounded the building, letting no one enter or exit. The water supply was cut off and the latrines were soon overflowing. Worst of all, there was hardly anything to eat. It was Passover, but the uninvited guests occupying the Jewish community center of Trieste were offered no bread of affliction, neither unleavened nor leavened. Concentration camp survivors were accustomed to much worse conditions, and so they endured the festival week in the increasingly fetid building.

On the seventh day of Passover, Jews traditionally commemorate the delivery of their ancestors from captivity in Egypt due to the miraculous parting of the Red Sea. As diverse as the throng confined to the Trieste community center was, everyone was focused in his own way on the theme of escape from captivity. Some young men of Hassidic background re-enacted the crossing of the Red Sea in vivid (if unintentionally comic) fashion by taking turns leaping over a washtub filled with water.

On the eighth and final day of Passover, Jews have always remembered their dead by reciting the *Yizkor* prayer. For Judit, as for most of those in the building that day, this was the first opportunity for such a commemoration. Much as she wanted to honor the memory of her beloved parents and brothers, she found herself overwhelmed by anguish. It was still too fresh, too raw. Objectively speaking, she knew the tragic facts, but something within her recoiled at the thought of reciting the same prayer as countless generations of bereaved Jews before her. Less than a year earlier in Schwerin, when the girls who had survived Auschwitz lit the *Shavuos* candles in defiance of the curfew, Judit was still hoping that her family had somehow remained alive. By now, there was no longer any warrant for optimism. She simply could not bring herself to participate in the *Yizkor* service, and she turned away.

All the while, the *Bricha,* the Jewish underground organization that sought to smuggle people through the British blockade into *Eretz Yisrael,* was working feverishly to secure the group's release. At long last, a representative entered the building and told the people to leave calmly and quietly, but then proceed individually, as quickly as possible, to the train station. Once again, the right palms had been greased. At the station, the refugees boarded a train to *Milano* (Milan). They were told that they would be "taken care of" there. No tickets were necessary. On the train, they encountered a large group of youngsters who had survived without their parents, singing Zionist pioneer songs in loud and lusty Hebrew. Everyone joined in with great enthusiasm. What a wonderful feeling of camaraderie, of community! After two millennia of exile, the Jewish people were finally returning to their homeland.

In the middle of the night, word flashed through the train that the authorities were going to seize the Jewish passengers and deport them back to their countries of origin. In a panic, they all grabbed their knapsacks and jumped off the moving train into the darkness. It was a scene of sheer chaos, but by morning, saner heads prevailed. After what these people had all been through, a little paranoia was quite understandable; but Italy was now a free country, and no one was going to be sent anywhere against their will. The members of the Hungarian group eventually reassembled at the nearest train station and continued on, discreetly and undisturbed, to Milano. On the advice of other Jewish refugees they encountered in the street, they made their way to the offices of the United Nations Relief and Rehabilitation Administration (UNRRA), where, upon completing the required forms, they were officially registered as "displaced persons."

After a few days in Milano, they were notified that they would be going to the newly established Displaced Persons' Camp in Grugliasco, just outside Torino. Obviously, this was not where they wanted to be, nor was it UNRRA's intention that they stay there indefinitely. Yet, although it was far from clear what the future held for them, Judit and Béla, along with everyone else in the group, were relieved to be arriving at long last to a friendly resting place.

Grugliasco

The homeless Hungarian Jews found their sanctuary at the unimaginatively named "UNRRA Camp No. 17," joining the three thousand or so people already there. The camp had been established shortly before the group's arrival, on the grounds of the *Istituto Interprovinciale per Inferme di Mente*, (the Inter-Provincial Institute for the Infirm of Mind), which had originally housed an all-female psychiatric hospital.

The United Nations Relief and Rehabilitation Administration had been created in 1943 to help countries occupied by Germany during the Second World War. Its two major functions were relief activities in the liberated countries and caring for displaced persons in camps set up for this purpose. The term "displaced persons," favored by the administrators, suggested that the people in question had been nudged out of their old homes in as neutral a fashion as the water had been nudged out of Archimedes' famous bathtub. In reality, they were refugees.

Jews accounted for approximately a quarter of all the refugees entrusted to UNRRA. It is interesting to note that the camps were established in Germany, Austria, and Italy, which strongly suggests that they were a form of punishment inflicted by the victors upon the vanquished. Those who had caused the War leading to the problem of the refugees could now squirm at having these wretched people deposited in their very midst. Some UNRRA facilities were actually established on the grounds of former concentration camps, without regard to the sensitivities of those who had just been liberated from those hellish places.

The camps were meant to provide a short-term housing solution for people uprooted from their homes after the War. In practice, many of the camps became longer-term domiciles for Jews who refused to return to their native lands because of bad memories or rampant anti-Semitism, but were unable to emigrate to *Eretz Yisrael* or North America because of stringent immigration restrictions.

Early in the War, the Italian army had requisitioned the residential quarters of the *Istituto Interprovinciale per Inferme di Mente* for the billeting of troops stationed in the area. All of the patients were relocated to other psychiatric establishments in the north of Italy. An order of nuns originally assigned to care for the all-female patients maintained a convent in a building at the entrance to the campus. After the departure of their charges, the sisters expressed the wish to stay on, and the fascists permitted them to remain in order to pursue the contemplative life. Upon the collapse of Mussolini's government and the German seizure of Italy, members of the *Wehrmacht* replaced the Italian soldiers in the Grugliasco dormitories.

The end of the War brought British military occupation. The campus was first handed to the British Red Cross, and then to UNRRA. The nuns continued to practice their tranquil ways, oblivious to the never-ending turmoil raging around them, and stoically enduring their latest neighbors.

The buildings no doubt functioned well enough when utilized for their originally intended purpose. However, they did not stand up to the extraordinary demands now being made on them. The camp's population far exceeded the numbers the buildings were designed to accommodate. Bedrooms meant for four psychiatric patients of the same gender now housed seven married couples. Some residents tried to improvise privacy partitions out of the flimsy camp-issued blankets, but to little avail. Every whisper, every groan was clearly audible to their roommates.

As there were no storage facilities in the rooms, residents had to keep their personal belongings stowed in bags beneath their beds.

The hopelessly inadequate toilet and shower facilities were clustered at either end of the long, narrow hallways. They had intentionally been built without partitions so that the staff could keep the all-female patients under constant surveillance.

As people had to sleep together and go to the bathroom together, it is not surprising that they had to eat together as well. Each dormitory room was furnished with a long wooden table with benches on either side. At mealtimes, residents picked up their food from the central kitchen and brought it back to their rooms.

The complete lack of privacy and personal space made people even more irritable than they already had good reason to be. There was constant arguing and bickering.

Married couples in Grugliasco had a strong incentive to start a family: those fortunate enough to have children were assigned to one of the special smaller rooms, which had previously held dangerous psychiatric patients in solitary confinement. They did not have more personal space in these claustrophobic quarters than in the wards, but they did have precious privacy.

The only others to receive private accommodations were the handful of residents known to have served as *Kapos*, privileged prisoners put in charge of groups of other Jewish prisoners in the concentration camps. These ruthless and conniving people had always managed to obtain the best of everything for themselves at the expense of others. They were able to ingratiate themselves with the British administrators of the camp and gain special consideration, just as they had done with the German administrators of the concentration camps. Such was the power of the *Kapos* over their fellow Jews that, even now, no one was willing to challenge them. All the *Kapos* were of Polish origin. The Jews of Poland had been the first to fall under German occupation, and thus they were the earliest inmates in the concentration camps. By the time the Hungarians and others arrived toward the end of the War, a small number among the Polish Jews who were still alive were well ensconced in positions of power.

The East European Jews comprising the majority of Grugliasco residents, who conversed in Yiddish, tended to have little use for those who did not, generally treating them with scornful contempt, and regarding them as having gotten off easily during the War.

All the residents of the camp were Jewish – except for a small group of Croats. These people kept a low profile and presented themselves as anti-Communists fearful of the Red Army now occupying their homeland. In reality, they were members of the Nazi-collaborationist Ustashi party that tyrannized wartime Croatia. They surmised correctly that a refugee camp full of Jews would be the ideal hiding place. The Jewish residents seem to have had no awareness of their neighbors' brutal, sadistic zeal in hunting down and murdering the Jews of Croatia.

There were also some Jews in the camp under false pretenses. These people never endured the hell of the concentration camps but arranged to have numbers tattooed on their forearms after the War. They did this in order to qualify for the special benefits from the Red Cross and other aid agencies available to camp survivors.

There was little evidence in the camp of either sickness or mortality. Those who had survived the War, after all, were the young and strong. The camp had a well-equipped infirmary staffed by a full-time English doctor, but there was little activity there. In the rare case of a serious medical condition, the patient would be transferred to a proper hospital in Torino. In the still less common instance of a patient dying in the hospital, funeral arrangements were made by the Torino Jewish community, and burial took place in the city's Jewish cemetery. Aside from the deceased's family, no one was interested in knowing about such occurrences, much less in traveling from Grugliasco for a funeral: The residents of the camp had all experienced quite enough of death. For the sake of facilitating their psychic healing, they chose to be in denial regarding this particular unpleasant aspect of life.

Each day, UNRRA provided the camp residents with food rations. They did nothing to deserve this; the food simply descended upon them like the Manna that had sustained their ancestors in the desert. However, unlike the Manna, which according to Jewish tradition took on whatever taste an individual imagined, the camp rations were decidedly unappetizing. They were also lacking in variety and balance. The dietary staple, as might have been expected in Italy, was pasta, pasta, and more pasta. The high-carbohydrate diet also contained a great deal of American-style white bread. To Europeans accustomed to full-bodied Pumpernickel, this tasted like cardboard. Once a day, the residents were served some kind of meat. The authorities also distributed a daily ration of unfiltered cigarettes to each resident, evidently regarding these as a basic human necessity. Although they were forbidden to do so, some non-smoking individuals traded their cigarettes for white bread, which they smuggled out of the camp along with their own hoarded slices. The routine consisted of certain men leaving the camp, ostensibly to go for a walk, and standing outside the high stone wall surrounding the grounds while their womenfolk on the inside tossed small bagsful of the bread over the top of the wall. The men caught the bags, put them together in large sacks, and took them to the open-air market in Torino, where they were able to sell the "American" white bread to very hungry Italians. The general population suffered widespread shortages of food after the War, but lacked the good fortune of having UNRRA to feed them. After a number of such illicit transactions, the enterprising black-marketers would have enough money to buy a scrawny chicken.

In the beginning, UNRRA had assigned a *shoichet*, a Jewish ritual slaughterer, to provide for the religious needs of the tiny minority of Grugliasco residents who kept kosher. This arrangement did not last very long. When the *shoichet* was withdrawn from the camp, he left behind the ink-stamp that he had applied to the chickens he slaughtered. The Hebrew lettering below the UNRRA logo proclaimed that the bird bearing the stamp was kosher.

Fresh fruits and vegetables were simply not part of the camp diet. As a result, many people suffered from scurvy. In addition, the scarcity of dairy products resulted in calcium deficiencies. The poor diet had a particularly adverse impact on people who had arrived in Grugliasco already debilitated by years of malnutrition. Still, as much as they complained about the food, the residents could not help keeping things in perspective. Most of them deeply appreciated the fact that well-intentioned strangers were taking the trouble to feed them, even if their hardened circumstances prevented them, at times, from expressing their appreciation appropriately.

Of the couples in the Hungarian group, only Béla and Magdi Zimmerman and Jeno and Borika Schwarcz had arrived in Italy already married. A hasty double ceremony had been performed in the Rubinstein home in Szentistvan just before the even hastier departure of the entire group from Hungary. For the others, the urgent priority had been to get out of the country while this was still possible. Once they came to rest in Grugliasco, however, all thoughts turned to marriage. Indeed, it would seem that weddings were the primary social activity in the camp. The lack of opportunity to marry during the War had resulted in a huge pent-up demand, which was released in an enormous burst of matrimonial energy once life began returning to normal. Aside from the universal human impulses, for people whose families had been destroyed there was a special urgency and a sublime significance to creating new families.

Dezso and Vera Rubinstein and Sanyi and Kicsi Hofstadter were married along with five other couples in an assembly-line wedding on May 1, 1946. The venue was the religious Zionist "*kibbutz*" in the village of Abbiate, an hour's train ride from Grugliasco. Dezso, the great romantic of the group, wanted to do something special for his bride. He hired a boy with a bicycle pulling a three-wheeled cart to transport Vera from the train station into Abbiate, while he strode solemnly alongside. All of the celebrants were wearing the best clothes in their extremely limited wardrobes. A single gray veil was passed from one bride to the next, as the *kibbutz* rabbi performed ceremony after ceremony. At the end, all of the guests sat down with the *kibbutz* members for a special wedding feast of rice pudding. There were no flowers on the tables; there were not even tablecloths. Yet, the joy of the celebrants was indescribable. For years, none of them had experienced a Jewish wedding. There was a sense of triumphal defiance about it, as if they were proclaiming to their enemies: "You thought you could destroy us, you thought you could rob us of our humanity? Look! Not only have we Jews survived you, but we are making weddings!"

Practically every married woman in the camp capable of bearing a child was either pregnant or a new mother. There was a strong desire to make up for lost time. During the War, hardly any Jewish children were born, and amongst those who had been born, there was a very slight chance of survival. Moreover, the best antidote to the profound demoralization afflicting the survivors was to bring as many Jewish children as possible into the world, both to replace those who had been murdered and as an act of defiance against the vanquished murderers. The oldest child in the camp was Lonya, the adorable blond son of Sonia from Lithuania. She had given birth to him while hiding in the forest just before the War ended. Lonya was such a chronological oddity in Grugliasco that he became the camp mascot.

Béla and Judit never enjoyed a courtship in the common sense familiar to the great majority of people fortunate enough to live normal lives. When they decided to marry, while still in Hungary, their single-minded focus was on getting safely out of the country. They were hardly in a proper frame of mind for romance so soon after enduring their personal tragedies. Survivors like them tended to regard life as a grim and somber affair. Marriage was far more about the perpetuation of decimated families than about loving relationships between men and women. The people who were to become my parents were also exasperated by their restrictive situation. Although they were engaged to be married and had all the time in the world to act on this fact while idling in the camp, a serious obstacle burdened them. Béla required special rabbinical dispensation to remarry, since there were no eyewitnesses to confirm the presumed death of his wife in the gas chambers. The situation was tragically common in those days, and although the rabbis were highly sympathetic and eager to help, they had a huge backlog of cases to work through.

One day, Judit received word through a former neighbor that Rabbi Lemberger from Szerencs, who had known her family well and who was himself now a refugee, had just arrived in Livorno. Béla immediately traveled there and related his predicament to the rabbi. He returned to Grugliasco in high spirits, bearing a writ of dispensation attesting that, from what the undersigned had learned of the tragic circumstances, there was no reasonable doubt that Ibolya Rubinstein had been put to death in the gas chambers, and that therefore, Béla Rubinstein was free to marry Judit Schwarcz.

The wedding took place on Sunday, June 9, 1946, in the field next to the main building of the Grugliasco camp. Officiating at the marriage ceremony was a rabbi from Yugoslavia affiliated with the religious Zionist Mizrachi Organization. He was a fellow resident of Grugliasco waiting his turn to leave for *Eretz Yisrael*. The *kesubah*, the traditional Jewish marriage contract, was hand-written on a cheap piece of lined writing paper.

Everyone in the camp was invited to attend the wedding. Béla had bought a barrel of sardines in the market to share with the wedding guests in honor of the special occasion. Someone pulled out a harmonica, and the dancing and merriment continued late into the night under a starry Piedmontese sky.

Béla and Judit's wedding stood out because it was the only one to take place that day in Grugliasco.

Judit's instinctive reaction to the deep spiritual malaise gripping virtually everyone in the camp was to yearn for the stability and contentment she had known in her parents' traditional Jewish home. After marrying Béla, she decided to focus on *taharas hamishpachah*, literally "purity of the family." Jewish law requires a married woman to immerse herself in a *mikvah*, a ritual bath, every month following her menstrual cycle. If Sabbath observance was rare after the War, adherence to *taharas hamishpachah* was virtually non-existent. It was remarkable that Judit chose to cling so tenaciously to this particular commandment, considering how difficult it was to carry out in her circumstances.

Each month, she took the lonely train ride from Grugliasco to Milano, to the *mikvah* located in the Jewish communal building at Via Unione 5. As Jewish law permitted immersion in the *mikvah* only after nightfall, it was invariably too late to take the train back. Judit often spent the night sleeping on the floor with the latest group of refugee arrivals, awaiting their camp assignments, and returned to Grugliasco the following morning.

Judit was asked many years later why she had to travel all the way to Milano. Was there not a *mikvah* in Torino, near at hand? She responded that this possibility had never occurred to her. She simply did not know any observant Jews in Torino with whom she could have discussed the matter.[1]

In the years following the end of the Second World War, Italy was economically devastated. There was not nearly enough work for the Italians, let alone for the refugees in their midst. It was made clear to the residents of the Grugliasco camp that all their basic needs would be met, but they were forbidden to seek any kind of employment outside the camp. Those who had an entrepreneurial background and a strong work ethic were frustrated and humiliated to be sitting around day after day with nothing to do.

A Jewish woman in Torino, Signora Finzi, owned a small factory for the manufacture of leather purses and handbags. Motivated by sympathy for her co-religionists, she offered some of the Grugliasco residents unpaid employment, in order to teach them a trade. Béla, Dezso, and Sanyi were among the fortunate few selected for the privilege of working gratis for Signora Finzi. They appreciated the opportunity to be involved in productive activity that restored their sense of dignity. They also learned how to use a sharp razor to cut pieces of leather. At the time, they could not possibly have imagined how useful this skill would one day prove to be.

When the anti-Jewish laws had been passed in Hungary before the War, Jews were banned from attending public school. Judit had been an eager student with an insatiable thirst for knowledge, and she was extremely upset about being prevented from pursuing her education. For a while, her father was able to pay a Jewish woman, who had been dismissed from her teaching position under the new laws, to tutor her privately at home. But he had lost his own job as a teacher, and the money soon ran out. Feeling deeply the pain of his daughter, Eliahu Schwarcz took her on long walks and urged her to ask him any question she liked, on any topic. It seemed to Judit that he was never at a loss to provide a satisfactory answer. However, it was a difficult time, and what was needed was practical education. Her mother arranged for Judit to work for a Jewish dressmaker, at least to learn a useful trade.

This, too, would prove to be a good thing. The Organization for Rehabilitative Training (ORT), with support from the American Jewish Joint Distribution Committee (AJJDC), was active in Grugliasco, as it was in many other refugee camps. ORT established workshops that taught metalworking, woodworking, and leather tanning to the men, and dressmaking and knitting to the women. All the machinery, materials, and manuals came from headquarters in Switzerland. When ORT officials learned that Judit was an experienced dressmaker, they offered her a job as an instructor in the design and sewing of dresses. She was assigned thirty-nine students, mostly simple women from primitive backgrounds. The first time she let them work on the non-electric, foot-pedal-operated sewing machine, they were frightened. But they were happy to be learning a trade, and grateful for an activity to fill their empty days. Judit, in turn, was happy to be doing something productive, and she certainly appreciated the modest ORT salary. She used the money to buy fresh fruits and vegetables at the market, supplementing the nutritionally limited camp diet. Judit was eventually promoted to the position of vice-president of the Grugliasco chapter. Her new job consisted of visiting women in the camp who had recently given birth, and advising them on how to care for their babies. These women did not have mothers of their own to guide them, and they tended to be overprotective because of their own vulnerable pasts. Judit continued working for ORT until she was ready to give birth to her own child.

In addition to supporting the activities of ORT, the AJJDC was active in Grugliasco in its own right. Every year before Rosh Hashanah, in accordance with tradition, it delivered a bag of almonds and raisins to each family. Everyone appreciated this small but thoughtful gesture of Jewish solidarity. However, what really made a practical difference to the lives of people in the camp were the huge bales of used clothing that arrived periodically from the United States. Particularly prized were baby layettes and winter clothes. Camp residents were touched to realize that total strangers in distant America cared about them as fellow Jews and went to the effort of helping them.

There was not nearly enough activity in the camp to keep people happy. The combination of long-term idleness and lack of privacy resulted in a very high level of frustration. Residents whose nerves were frayed by their wartime ordeals bickered and argued with one another at the slightest provocation.

The authorities made a conscientious effort to provide for Jewish religious needs. They naïvely assumed that those who had endured the hell of the concentration camps would be driven to seek solace in their ancestral faith. A synagogue was established and equipped with a brand-new Torah scroll and prayer books. The well-meaning Englishmen running the camp, with their serene Anglican sensibility, simply did not comprehend the fury of these Jews against the God who had abandoned them at the moment of their most desperate need. Hardly anyone attended the Friday evening prayer services. On weekdays, there was no demand at all for services, and the synagogue was kept locked.

On those festival days when the traditional *Yizkor* prayer was recited in memory of loved ones, virtually everyone lit long candles and showed up at the synagogue, but only for the brief memorial portion of the service. A torrent of emotions rushed forth, a wail of lamentation engulfing the camp as the all-too-raw recent tragedy of the Jewish people was recalled. Then, emotionally exhausted, and embarrassed by this relapse into the discredited old ways, the residents stumbled out of the synagogue and back to their nihilistic despair.

Hardly anyone in the camp was interested in lectures or classes on Judaism. On the other hand, the old Hollywood films screened every Thursday night always drew a full house.

Zionist movements representing the entire spectrum from revisionist to labor and from religious to atheist, invested great efforts in reaching out to the Jews of Grugliasco, regarding them, quite naturally, as prospective citizens of the nascent Jewish state. Although they worked together toward the common goal of convincing people to go to *Eretz Yisrael*, the various movements also competed vigorously amongst themselves to attract recruits. The debates got quite heated at times, and took on the character of a spectator sport. Fans would crowd around to cheer their "team," grateful for the spirited alleviation of boredom. The small number of Hungarian Jews in the camp felt marginalized by these debates, which were always conducted in Yiddish. It was not only that their grasp of the Yiddish language was so poor; there was also a vast cultural chasm between the Hungarians, who were culturally Austro-Hungarian even when they were religiously observant, and the Eastern Europeans, who were culturally Jewish even when they were religiously alienated.

By and large, these were embittered, demoralized, cynical people, deeply scarred by the horrors they had endured. Very few things had the capacity to inspire them. Zionism, however, had a special resonance for those who had suffered the tragic consequences of Jewish powerlessness. They tingled with excitement at the prospect of Jews finally taking control of their destiny in their own state.

The basic human need of the Grugliasco residents for shelter and sustenance was quite well met. But it was far easier to heal the body than it was to heal the spirit. In the early days after arriving at the camp, Béla Rubinstein was detached and distant. For long hours, he would lie on his bed in the dormitory, staring blankly at the ceiling. Everyone left him alone, understanding that he had still not made his peace with the loss of his family. It would be some time yet before he was interested in doing anything other than mourn his loved ones.

Judit Rubinstein, for her part, craved companionship. She too had lost her family, although not a spouse and children. Her way of dealing with the pain, in keeping with her sociable nature, was to reach out to other people. Her husband's family became her own. She was particularly close to her brother-in-law Armin, who served as patriarch to the little group. He was a wise, empathetic person, reminding Judit of her own father, and she was grateful to him for his guidance and friendship. The two of them would go for long, leisurely walks around Grugliasco, discussing everything under the sun, usually ending up at the small café near the camp where they would drink a glass of cold milk.

Judit, along with Armin and Béla Zimmerman, decided to travel to Rome to see the great city. The only problem was that they had no money for train tickets. Someone hit upon the brilliant idea of imprinting ticket-sized pieces of paper with the kosher meat stamp left behind by the ritual slaughterer. When the ticket collector came by, they handed over their homemade tickets. The poor fellow contorted his face in puzzlement and scratched his head, recognizing the UNRRA logo but mystified by the strange markings below it. He let the travelers stay on the train, and they assumed that he took pity on them because they were refugees. They understood the ticket collector's reaction as characteristically Italian, demonstrating a basic civility and sense of common humanity.

The residents of UNRRA Camp No. 17 experienced many such acts of kindness by ordinary Italians. They came to regard these gestures as vital to the gradual restoration of their faith in humankind.

Not long after arriving in Grugliasco, my mother met a local woman by the name of Franca who owned a sewing machine. Upon learning that she was a seamstress, Franca encouraged her to use the machine to sew herself a dress. Grateful to experience such generosity, my mother sewed her new friend an identical dress. Franca jabbered endlessly in rapid-fire Italian, complaining bitterly about her husband's abusiveness and infidelity. My mother had only a vague idea of what she was saying, but it did not really matter. The important thing was that she had succeeded in establishing a personal relationship with a complete outsider who proved to be a warm and caring human being.

My mother recalls with particular approbation the time, shortly after I was born, she had to take me to a pediatrician in Torino for my first check-up. Finding herself hopelessly lost in the unfamiliar streets, she showed the slip containing the doctor's address to a passing stranger, and asked if he could kindly point her in the right direction. Without hesitation, the gentleman took her by the arm, accompanied her onto a tram for a ten-minute ride, and then walked with her for several blocks, finally depositing mother and child at the entrance to the medical office.

Manifestations of decency were not limited to the local Italian populace. To this day, my mother retains fond memories of Miss Hayward, a native of Manchester who served as the personal assistant to Captain Davidge, the British administrator of the Grugliasco camp. (Surely she had a Christian name, but it was never revealed to the camp residents.) Miss Hayward was an exceptionally kind and compassionate individual. Horrified to learn of the barbarous atrocities committed against the Jews of Europe, she dedicated herself to atoning for the collective sins of the civilized world by tending as best she could to the needs of the surviving remnant.

Little by little, the suffocating darkness of the war years began to dissipate. It remained an incontrovertible fact that there were many evil people in the world. But day by day, it grew ever more apparent that there were plenty of good people as well. The spiritual lift provided by periodic encounters with members of the latter category gave the survivors reason to hope for a better future.

The War may have been over, but its aftershocks bedeviled many of the emotionally fragile residents of Grugliasco for a long time to come. The camp was brimming with heart-rending tragedies.

Eva was one of the women who worked with Judit as a sewing instructor. She had heard through the Maidanek grapevine that her husband Marek, her first and true love, was seen being led to the gas chamber. In her desperate loneliness and her craving to return to a normal life, she hastily married Berel, a fellow refugee. He was much older than she, and they had almost nothing in common. She bore two children by her new husband. One day, Marek showed up in Grugliasco, having somehow miraculously survived the gas chamber. Eva was exultant. Without hesitation, she abandoned Berel and her two children, and left the camp with Marek. Alas, Marek was no longer the person she had known and loved. His harrowing concentration camp experiences had thoroughly traumatized him, rendering him manic depressive and abusive. In truth, Eva was not the same person she had been six years earlier either. Within two weeks, she was back in Grugliasco with her new family.

There was a Czech couple, Clara and Haim, who for a brief time occupied the beds next to the Rubinsteins in the dormitory. Separated during the War, Clara ended up in France and Haim in Italy. Through mutual friends, each learned that the other had survived. Overjoyed, they experienced an emotional reunion in Grugliasco. Clara soon became pregnant with their first child. How eagerly they anticipated parenthood, after waiting so long! However, cruel fate was to deny them happiness, when complications set in and Clara died during childbirth. The baby survived, while Haim collapsed emotionally, and he was utterly incapable of caring for his child. Clara's sister came from France and took the little girl away. Every person in the camp felt the agony of the disconsolate father.

A particularly poignant and painful Grugliasco story concerned a member of the family. One day, Judit was astonished to learn that her cousin Artur, the son of her uncle Moishe, had arrived in the camp. His fair skin, blond hair, and penetrating blue eyes had enabled Artur to survive the War by passing as a Magyar. In the grim struggle for endurance, masquerading as a gentile was a perfectly sound strategy for those Jews fortunate enough to have the right looks. The problem was that Artur had taken his pretense a step too far by joining the viciously anti-Semitic Arrow Cross militia. When the War came to an end, this formerly useful deceit was suddenly a liability, and the seasoned opportunist reverted to his Jewish identity.

Fate swept Artur into the Grugliasco displaced persons' camp, precipitating an awkward encounter with his cousins. He could hardly bear to face them. He soon developed a reputation in the camp as an aggressive gambler and a hard drinker. Deeply troubled by this and unable to restrain herself, Judit told Artur that his conduct was reflecting very badly on the rest of the family. She urged him to remember what kind of home he came from, and to think how unhappy his martyred parents would be to see him carrying on like this. He retorted angrily: "My dear cousin, don't tell *me* what to do! I have blood on my hands, and I know this stinking world far better than *you* ever will. You people can stay in this crazy-house, but *I* have had more than enough!"

Soon afterwards, Artur disappeared from the camp. The word was that he had departed to Canada, under the sponsorship of the European Youth Immigration Program for orphaned survivors. As the story went, he eventually found his way to a small town in northern Quebec. There he lived a solitary and miserable life, until, in a tragically ironic twist, he came to a premature end in the local psychiatric hospital.

Certain residents of the camp proved unable to leave the less savory aspects of their wartime experiences behind them, and so managed to draw the enmity of the others. A prime example was Mr. Lobel, who had been assigned the job of camp postmaster. Every day, he sorted the incoming mail and distributed it to the addressees. It was common practice for relatives in other countries to send small amounts of money by mail to people in the camp. However, the envelopes were frequently delivered with obvious signs of tampering and relieved of their monetary contents. Judit once received a letter from her Aunt Malvina in Pittsburgh, referring to an enclosed gift of two dollars, but containing no trace of the cash. After a while, it became widely known that Lobel was helping himself to the money. Some people were so incensed that they grabbed the thief, held him captive in a room, and roughed him up. Civility ultimately prevailed, Lobel was let go, and he and his wife disappeared from the camp. The rumor spread that the Lobels made their way to America, where they could buy anonymous respectability with their ill-gotten gains.

Other residents would be caught red-handed stealing food rations from their fellows. They would grin nervously and offer the excuse that they were hungry. Still others broke into the general supply warehouse and appropriated things for themselves, using the concentration camp euphemism "*organisieren*," scraping together, to rationalize their theft. They could not grasp the moral distinction between outwitting the Nazis in order to survive and cheating their fellow Jews now that danger had passed. The self-obsessed behavior that had enabled them to endure the death camps was so deeply ingrained in their personalities that they were now enslaved by it.

The memory of concentration camps and forced labor camps was still vivid in the minds of the people in Grugliasco. To expect them to behave in a courteous and considerate manner so soon after the War would have been unreasonable, and perhaps even cruel. The exceptions to such behavior were remarkable.

Life in Grugliasco was anything but normal. However, it was a huge improvement over what all of the residents had just recently left behind them. They were not really free, but they were no longer enslaved. A curfew was in effect, and everyone was expected to be within the walls of the camp between 8:00 P.M. and 7:00 A.M. During the day, everyone was at liberty to do as they pleased – as long as they did not seek work. No one ever asked the residents where they were going or what they were doing. True, it was degrading for them not to be able to support themselves, but their basic need for shelter and sustenance was satisfied, and there were no enemies threatening their very existence. These were things that no survivor of the wartime camps could ever take for granted.

My father joked with the others that one day they would at last be settled somewhere, working hard for a living. They would look back with nostalgia to the carefree time in Grugliasco when they were on a perpetual vacation.

In the meantime, the residents of the Grugliasco camp began to reassemble the shattered pieces of their lives. Ever so gradually, they started to cultivate the commonplace aspirations of people everywhere. They dreamt of establishing households and raising children, of working with dignity and taking the occasional family trip.

My mother has often remarked that she is not sure how well the members of the group would have managed had they been given the opportunity to return to living a normal life right away. At the time, all they could think about was how irritated they were to be trapped in such a dreadful place after the torments they had just recently endured. In retrospect, it proved a great blessing that the survivors were granted this transitional breathing space before having to readjust to life in the outside world.

Torino / Toronto

T he nations of the world showed no enthusiasm for absorbing Jewish refugees after the War. This continued to be the case even after the grim facts concerning the Nazis' "Final Solution to the Jewish Problem" became widely known. The UNRRA camps were teeming with frustrated Jews who yearned for the opportunity to live normal, settled lives.

Many of the people in the camps, particularly those in Italy, wanted to go to Palestine, as it was then known. The experience of Jewish powerlessness had transformed them into ardent Zionists, determined to live in a sovereign Jewish state that could protect them from their enemies.

The situation was complex: the British government had capitulated to Arab pressure, and the Royal Navy was blockading the coast of Palestine to keep Jews out. Yet, the very same British government was charged with administering camps for Jewish refugees such as the one in Grugliasco, which happened to be located within their zone of occupation. A rather peculiar, and quite fascinating, tension between British *Realpolitik* and British civility was playing itself out.

All the Zionist organizations assigned *shlichim,* emissaries, to the camps in Italy. Overtly, the *shlichim* gave classes in conversational Hebrew and taught people to sing pioneer songs and dance the *hora.* Covertly, they worked feverishly to get their brethren out of the camps and into Palestine.

Captain Schlesinger was stationed in Grugliasco as a member of the Jewish Brigade, a unit in the British army. His official assignment was to facilitate communication between the English-speaking British administrators and the mostly Yiddish-speaking residents of the camp. From time to time, individuals would disappear overnight, and knowing glances would be exchanged the following morning. Everyone knew that those missing from roll call had been hidden by Schlesinger in the back of his army jeep and driven to the port of *Genova* (Genoa) to try their luck at running the British blockade. Those who stayed behind silently wished them success, and patiently waited their own turn. The irony of the situation was not lost on anyone, least of all the British military officer, Captain Schlesinger.

The most fervent Zionists in the family were Borika and Jeno. The only member of the group who came from an assimilated background, Jeno repeatedly told the others that after what had happened in Europe, it was impossible for him to remain a Jew unless he lived in a Jewish state. Eventually, Borika and Jeno's opportunity arrived. However, the British intercepted their boat before it could land on the Mediterranean shore, and they were taken to a detention camp in Cyprus. Their son Yehoshua was born there, and they finally reached their destination a year later, after the establishment of the State of Israel.

My parents were among those awaiting their own opportunity. My mother yearned to go to *Eretz Yisrael* in fulfillment of her beloved father's final wish. She was also anxious to join Yitzchak, her only surviving brother, who was already there. Like so many others, Yitzchak had sworn that he would never again live in a country where Jews were at the mercy of their enemies.

A serious complication arose along the way: I was born in March 1948, and the armies of the five neighboring Arab countries invaded the newly proclaimed State of Israel just two months later. There was no longer a British blockade to worry about, but immigrants disembarking in Haifa could expect to have weapons thrust into their hands and to be sent directly to the front lines. Families with small children were deemed to be an unwieldy burden in this latest Jewish struggle for survival.

Shortly afterward, a different opportunity arose, to go instead to a remote but peaceful country called Canada.

Judging by the historical record, Canada seemed a rather implausible haven for homeless Jews. In 1938, thirty-two nations including Canada had attended the Evian Conference to discuss the problem of Jewish refugees fleeing Nazi Germany. All of them decided to refuse further Jewish immigration. In 1939, the S.S. St. Louis, packed with German Jewish refugees, was denied sanctuary in Canada after being refused entry to Cuba and the United States, and forced to return to Europe. During the War, the leadership of the Canadian Jewish community tried desperately to convince the government to admit Jewish refugees beyond the very restrictive quota then in place. Throughout this period, Canada let in only about five thousand Jews – one of the worst records of any of the refugee-receiving countries.[1]

The basis of Canada's post-war immigration policy was contained in a statement issued by Prime Minister William Lyon Mackenzie King on May 1, 1947.[2] He declared that Canada would participate in the rescue and resettlement of displaced persons from the European camps. At the same time, he laid out the views of the government with regard to longer-term immigration policy. Immigrants would be selected carefully because admission to Canada was a privilege, not a right. The number of immigrants to be admitted would relate to the absorptive capacity of the country. Since absorptive capacity varies from year to year depending on economic conditions, the number of immigrants admitted in a given year would also vary.

What remained unstated by Mackenzie King was that in the government's view, Jews were undesirables who would strain the "absorptive capacity" of the country in *any* year. Thus, although it was clearly in the national interest to increase the population, it was also considered to be in the national interest to limit the number of Jewish immigrants to the bare minimum.

Today, Canadians cherish their well-earned image as a humane and compassionate nation. It is a sad historical reality, however, that as late as 1948, the government of Canada did not want to accept Jewish immigrants. Frederick Charles Blair, director of the Immigration Branch, faithfully enforced this policy. He warned that unless "safeguards" were put in place, there was a danger of Canada being "flooded with Jewish people." He made no secret of his personal dislike for Jews, and he was very proud of his strong record in keeping them out of Canada.[3] When asked by a delegation of Jewish community leaders how many Jews he would be prepared to see enter the country, an unidentified senior immigration official issued the infamous response that "none is too many".[41]

The leaders of the Jewish community concluded that the only way to get significant numbers of Jewish refugees into Canada was to demonstrate that they had something of value to contribute. The garment industry, for example, was a mainstay of the Canadian economy, but its growth was hampered by a chronic shortage of workers. As it happened, this industry was heavily represented by Jews at all levels, from business owners to union officials and workers. For once, they overcame their customary adversarial relationship in order to help their unfortunate brethren trapped in Europe. The Canadian Overseas Garment Commission, a partnership between the Canadian Jewish Congress and the Canadian Garment Workers' Union, was established to bring skilled tailors to Canada from the refugee camps. The Canadian Overseas Fur Commission followed soon afterwards.[5]

The politicians regarded the intensive lobbying in Ottawa as evidence of the well-known Jewish trait of "pushiness," but in the end, it paid off. In October 1947, approval was granted for the admission of two thousand one hundred thirty-six tailors and five hundred furriers. There was no specific mention of Jews in the Order-in-Council; from the government's point of view, this was to be a strictly pragmatic, economically motivated immigration.

An eight-man delegation, headed by Canadian Fur Workers' Union officials Harris Silver and Max Federman, came to Rome in June 1948 to recruit Jews from the various Italian refugee camps. Armin Rubinstein worked in the office of Captain Davidge, the British military administrator of the Grugliasco camp. Just before the arrival of the Canadians, Armin's boss informed him of the initiative and Armin immediately told his family.

It was mid-day on Friday, June 11. Interviews were going to be held on a first come, first served basis beginning Sunday, June 13, the first day of the *Shavuos* holiday. However, in order to get there in time, the men would have to desecrate the sanctity of *Shabbos* by riding the train to Rome on Saturday. They turned for guidance to Armin, who was an accomplished Talmudic scholar. He ruled that the situation was one of *pikuach nefesh,* a matter of life and death, and thus it was not only permissible, but actually mandatory, to travel to Rome to be interviewed by the Canadians.

When the three Rubinstein brothers, Armin, Béla, and Dezso, together with Sanyi Hofstadter and Béla Zimmerman, arrived at the appointed place in Rome, a long queue of aspiring furriers had already formed. They did manage, however, to be among those fortunate enough to be granted interviews. None of the men in the family had any experience working with furs, nor did the great majority of those standing in line with them. The Jewish officials from Canada had no difficulty figuring this out, but they did not care: whatever the views of their government, *they* were on a humanitarian mission to bring as many dispossessed Jews as possible to a better life in Canada.

For the purposes of the interview with the officials, the Rubinstein brothers pointed out that their late father, Mordechai, had been a dealer in animal pelts. This was nearly enough to qualify them, but the decisive factor was their ability to cut leather with a razor, a skill they had acquired along with Sanyi in Signora Finzi's handbag workshop. Béla, Dezso, and Sanyi were accepted. Armin was rejected because, at fifty-six, he was deemed too old to be of benefit to Canada. According to family lore, Béla Zimmerman was turned down because the delegation, interviewing the applicants in alphabetical order, had filled its quota long before it reached the final letter of the alphabet. A less frequently cited explanation is that he failed the medical examination because of scars left on a lung by a long-forgotten childhood illness.

By the following day, word of the interviews had spread through all the Italian camps, and a mob of Jewish refugees desperate to become Canadians descended upon Rome. Alas, the delegation's meager quota had already been filled the day before. Many latecomers were highly resentful. Believing that, as usual, his money could get him whatever he wanted, one of the Grugliasco black-marketers offered five thousand dollars in cash to any accepted applicant who was willing to switch identities. There were no takers.

The delighted new furriers were oblivious to the intrigue that had raged behind the scenes in faraway Ottawa. After much wheeling and dealing, the delegation was authorized to fill the five hundred-person furrier quota with three hundred Jews and two hundred non-Jews. The Canadian authorities regarded this ratio as a grand concession to the "pushy" Jews. They had at first insisted on an equal balance between Jews and non-Jews because they did not want the project to be regarded as a crafty scheme for Jews to jump the immigration queue. In the end, they grudgingly conceded that the split was not realistic, given the enormity of the Jewish refugee problem in Europe.

Sure enough, finding the Jews was easy; but only fifty-nine displaced gentiles interested in going to Canada as furriers could be identified by the delegation. After all, non-Jews were welcome in Canada, and had no end of employment opportunities. The displeased Canadian authorities abruptly halted the entire program. The delegation, they complained, had not kept its end of the bargain by adhering to the agreed-upon ratio. Harry Rubin and Joe Kerbel, representing the fur industry, met in Ottawa with the Deputy Minister of Labor and the Director of Immigration, and they were informed that no Jewish furriers would come to Canada until the quota of two hundred non-Jews was filled. At long last, the government authorized the recruitment of one hundred forty-one inexperienced non-Jewish single females between the ages of eighteen and twenty-five, who would come as apprentices to the fur industry.

A number of people questioned the wisdom of agreeing to what was in effect a *numerus clausus* with regard to Jewish immigration into Canada. There was also a certain uneasiness that some of the non-Jewish individuals coming to Canada might have been involved in war crimes against Jews. The leaders consoled themselves with the thought that while the one hundred forty-one non-Jewish women were coming as individuals, the three hundred Jewish men were coming with their families, for an actual total closer to eight hundred Jews redeemed from the refugee camps.[6]

The immigration authorities took great pride in their rigorous standards: only the very best people were to be allowed into Canada. Indeed, of the individuals approved by the recruitment delegation, over half were subsequently rejected on the grounds of bad health or bad politics. Official Tom Aplin crowed that only one known Communist slipped through the screening process. "As soon as we discovered his political sympathies, the RCMP was notified. I don't know where he is now. He certainly isn't in the factory."[7]

Béla Rubinstein, onetime secretary of the Szentistvan branch of the Hungarian Communist Party, must have been less than candid when questioned about his political background, for he did make it into the factory. The authorities need not have worried about this particular Jewish immigrant: no more ardent capitalist was to be found in the entire Dominion.

The very first group to be assembled for passage to Canada included my parents along with me, my Uncle Dezso and Aunt Vera and my cousin Annie. Priority was given to settling families with small children. Sanyi and Kicsi, and the other childless couples, were to follow a week later.

The travelers made their way to the port of Genova, and set sail on a dilapidated Polish cargo ship, the *S.S. Sobieski*, which should have been decommissioned years before the journey. The dimly lit, airless hold was crammed full of refugees, with men at the front and women and children in the back. The North Atlantic was particularly stormy and turbulent throughout the journey. As the ship lurched from side to side, the shipment of iron rods stowed overhead rolled about, crashing and clanging in a thunderous racket. It was virtually impossible to sleep. It was also very difficult to hold down food. Like most of the passengers, Vera was seasick all the way to Canada, and was unable to nurse Annie. My mother assumed the task of feeding Annie as well as me. By the fourth day, my mother also became so nauseous that she could not look at food. An unfamiliar stewardess showed up in the hold, took my mother by the hand, and led her to a cabin. On the table was a large plate of Italian noodles and a glass of wine. The stewardess ordered her to start eating, if she wished herself and the babies to be among the living when the ship arrived in Canada. She obeyed the order, and from that moment on, her appetite was restored. My mother never saw the stewardess again. To this day, she is convinced the benevolent stranger was a guardian angel sent from heaven to save her, so that she in turn could save Annie and me.

Finally, on September 19, 1948, my mother's twenty-seventh birthday, the *S.S. Sobieski* docked at Pier 21 in Halifax, the celebrated point of arrival for many generations of new immigrants to Canada. Representatives of the Canadian Fur Workers' Union were there to greet the newcomers and accompany them to the train station. They were presented with a choice of three cities boasting a fur industry: Montreal, Toronto, or Winnipeg. Most of the group got off in Montreal, perhaps in their impatience to put an end to the years of homelessness. The rest continued on to Toronto. Hardly anyone opted for the additional long ride to Winnipeg, which was reported to be too remote from civilization and too cold in the winter to be fit for human habitation. When family members pondered the Montreal option, language arose as an obstacle. My father made the point that it would be difficult enough for Hungarian speakers, notoriously poor students of foreign tongues, to master English, let alone

French, in the bilingual city. And so, they decided on Toronto. Besides, "Toronto" sounded rather like "Torino," and they eagerly grasped at the flimsiest hint of familiarity in this promising but alien land.

The train carrying the thirty-eight-member group of furriers-to-be and their families pulled into Union Station early in the morning of Wednesday, September 22, 1948. The very first such group to arrive in Toronto, they were greeted by Miss Tobie Taback, secretary of the Jewish Immigrant Aid Society of Canada (JIAS), and some employees of the United Jewish Relief Agencies, as well as an official from the Canadian Department of Immigration.

The Canadian Jewish Congress (CJC), working together with JIAS, had made a commitment to the Canadian government to provide the newcomers with accommodations. The immigration official was present at the train station that morning not so much to welcome the new arrivals to Canada as to ensure that they not set up camp in the manner of Gypsies. No one was permitted to leave the station before Miss Taback established that each person in the group had a place to live. It had not been easy for the CJC to arrange this: finding accommodations was a difficult challenge in those days of rapid population growth in Toronto. To complicate matters further, the landlords of the city were prepared to rent to adults, but few wanted to accept families with small children.

From the station, the travelers were taken to Goldenberg's Kosher Restaurant for breakfast. They were famished, as they had not been given anything to eat since leaving Montreal. They devoured the baskets of bread on the tables to the last crumb before the waitress could bring them their scrambled eggs and coffee. After breakfast, the group was taken to the Labor Lyceum for processing.

Once all the paperwork was completed, a CJC employee was assigned to accompany each family to its new home. My parents were led up a dark staircase to a dingy two-room apartment on the second floor of a badly rundown building at 90 McCaul Street. Before handing over the key, their chaperone explained in Yiddish that the CJC had already advanced the first month's rent to the landlord. My father was expected to repay this amount and to begin paying rent as soon as he started earning wages. His employer would withhold up to ten percent of his salary each month for this purpose, and remit it directly to the CJC, which was held responsible by the government for paying the landlord. To ensure that there would be no misunderstanding, my father had to sign a document spelling out the arrangement – in English, a language he did not yet comprehend.

The cockroaches were in command at 90 McCaul Street. A single bathroom served the needs of all five tenant families, as well as the "ladies" on the third floor and their visitors who clambered up and down the stairs at all hours of the day and night. The only furnishings in the apartment were a double bed and a crib. My mother stood silent, staring at the grimy walls, and sobbed to herself. She did not wish to give the impression that she was ungrateful to be in Canada, but she could not help thinking of her spotless home in Szerencs, of her parents, brothers, uncles, aunts, and cousins. She did not know anyone in this place, and she could not understand what the people were saying. *Is this how Canadians lived, in filthy, squalid apartments? Did she leave Hungary and endure being a refugee for almost three years in order to end up with this?*

My mother's first activity in Toronto was to get down on her hands and knees to scrub the floor. She was determined that her infant son would grow up with dignity in a clean home, however modest it might be.

As soon as she had stripped away the thick layer of grime encrusting the oven, she baked a traditional Hungarian *kokos* cake, just like those her own mother had baked at home. The neighbors could not help but notice the delicious aroma wafting out of the new tenants' apartment.

The following day, my parents strolled around the neighborhood to get a sense of their new habitat. As they did not yet have a baby carriage, they had to carry me in their arms. They were delighted to find a butcher shop displaying a sign with the Hebrew words *bassar kasher*, kosher meat, on College Street. They took this as an omen that perhaps, with some effort, the strange new city could actually become their home. In the wartime camps, it had been impossible to keep kosher: staying alive necessitated eating whatever food was available. After the War, my parents were determined to observe the Jewish dietary laws, in memory of their parents and as a matter of self-respect as Jews.

In the evening, there was a spirited knock on the door. *Who could it possibly be?* A large, redheaded woman in a floral print dress stood in the doorway. She thrust a huge bouquet of pink carnations at my parents. Smiling broadly, she introduced herself as Margaret. My parents were astonished: someone actually knew and cared that the Rubinsteins had arrived in Toronto! What wonderful people must live in this city, greeting total strangers with flowers and good wishes. My mother was deeply moved, but also embarrassed that she could not receive her first visitor graciously in the still quite filthy and unfurnished apartment. Margaret promised to look in on them regularly, and offered to help if they needed anything at all.

Two days later, on Saturday morning, my father and my Uncle Dezso set out in search of their fellow Jews. All their lives, except for the disruptive period of the War and its aftermath, they had attended synagogue services on *Shabbos,* and they were eager to re-synchronize with the rhythms of their past. They felt a need, in this unfamiliar new place, to develop a sense of rootedness, of belonging to a community. They knew there were Jews living in Toronto, but they had no idea where to find them. They wandered the streets until they spotted a well-dressed gentleman carrying a velvet prayer-shawl bag under his arm. My father asked the stranger whether he was going to *shul.* Yes, he was, and yes, they could follow him there if they wished.

The regulars at the synagogue were not very friendly to the strangers joining them for services. Poor newcomers from Europe were an increasingly common sight those days. *Who knew what these people might demand if they were shown some civility? Give them a hand and they will probably try to take your whole arm!*

A single individual among the congregants that day, Mr. Abraham Starkman, threw caution to the wind. He welcomed my father and uncle and invited them to his home for a traditional *Kiddush.* With a hearty *"l'chaim!"* (To life!) over a shot of rye whisky, followed by schmaltz herring and honey cake, the veteran wished the neophytes much success in their new life. This simple act of kindness from a total stranger had a greater impact on his guests than the host could possibly have imagined.

My father went home in elevated spirits and told my mother that there seemed to be some fine people in Toronto; they only needed to be found. In the afternoon, my parents went for a stroll around the neighborhood, which was already beginning to feel more familiar. They were crestfallen to discover that the butcher shop displaying the kosher meat sign was open for business on *Shabbos*, selling pastrami sandwiches to passersby from a table on the sidewalk. "Kosher" seemed to mean something rather different in Canada than it did in the old country.

They were in for another shock when a fellow Hungarian-speaking immigrant they met on the street warned them about Margaret. The friendly woman who had greeted them with flowers worked for the Scott Mission, whose director was a *meshumad,* an apostate named Dr. Morris Zeidman. Margaret's real agenda was to bring salvation through Christ to her fellow Jews.

The next time the now-unmasked missionary came to the door, my mother politely set her straight. Although she and her husband greatly appreciated her attentiveness, they were devoted to their own faith and had no intention of converting to another. They never saw Margaret again.

Yom Kippur, the holiest day of the year, came three weeks later. My mother was anxious to go to synagogue to recite the *Yizkor* memorial prayer for her parents. After her return from Auschwitz, she had been inconsolable. She tried to participate in *Yizkor* services, but her raging despair kept overwhelming her. To make matters worse, she felt guilty over her failure. But now that she and her family were finally free to live normal lives, my mother was determined to make her peace with God and honor the memory of her beloved parents in the manner they would have approved.

One of the neighbors promised that her daughter would come to baby-sit. When the young woman failed to show up, my mother had no choice but to take me with her as she walked to the nearest synagogue, on Henry Street. The only person who seemed to take notice of her presence there was the *gabbai,* the sexton, who gave her an icy stare. "Hey, lady!" he sneered. "Don't you know it is forbidden to bring babies into the *shul?* They make a racket and disturb the worshippers!" Mortified, my mother left the building in silence.

Back home, she was seized by a terrible loneliness, and she focused with all her might on praying for the souls of her parents. She was astonished that she had it in her, and even more astonished when she felt as if a heavy burden was being lifted from her. It was a great relief that what she thought was her spiritual death proved after all to have been merely a spiritual hibernation.

One of the very few people who took a genuine interest in my parents in the early days was Mrs. Lerner, a young widow with several small children who lived directly across the street. She ran a grocery store out of her living room to support her family. Although she had arrived from Poland many years before, she spoke only Yiddish. Having endured her own hard times, she empathized with the newcomers and served as their advisor on matters relating to life in Canada. She also helped them to furnish their bare apartment by providing them with orange crates from her grocery store, which they used for storage.

The Rubinsteins had no choice but to stay in that first apartment on McCaul for almost a year. As soon as they could afford it, they moved to a more livable place. Their new landlady, Mrs. Goldberg, had been living in Canada since the 1920's. She came from a primitive Polish village, and assumed that her new tenants were of a similar background. When she first showed them the apartment, she ceremoniously pointed out the flush toilet, explaining its purpose and demonstrating its operation. My parents nodded politely. Like the mysterious stewardess on the ship and like Mrs. Lerner, Mrs. Goldberg became a guardian angel to her personal newcomers. She boosted their morale with much-appreciated words of encouragement and concern. "If they tell you it is impossible to keep *Shabbos* in Canada, don't believe them. I did it, and so can you, if you want to."

In general, the immigrants encountered a real challenge in the attitudes of many members of the established community, which ranged from indifference to outright hostility. Morris and Rose Diamond, fellow immigrants from Hungary, rented their first apartment in Toronto, an attic hovel, for forty dollars a month. After a year, when their landlady came to appreciate what fine people they were, she acknowledged that forty dollars was an exorbitant amount of rent for such a humble habitat. She had really wanted old-timers as tenants, and had quoted the *greeners* this unrealistic rent in the hope of frightening them off. In the end, she was glad they had persisted.

Little by little, as my parents grew more financially secure, they were able to improve their material circumstances. They moved, once again, to a larger and more comfortable apartment with a substantial kitchen area. They decided to replace their old-fashioned icebox with an electrically-powered refrigerator. As the kitchen had never before been fitted with electrical appliances, it was necessary to wire in a receptacle. The landlord recommended Mr. Steinberg, an electrician who lived in the neighborhood. Mr. Steinberg asked my mother why she needed power in the kitchen. When she told him it was for a refrigerator, he exploded. "Ha! Look at that! You just arrived in this country, and already you bought a refrigerator? I have been here for thirty years and I still don't have one!"

Mr. Steinberg calmed down and installed the receptacle. Whatever he may have thought of the newcomers, their money was, after all, as good as anyone's.

This was a novel Canadian experience for the Rubinsteins. For the first time since their arrival, they were encountering jealousy from an old-timer whom they were leaving behind on their climb up the socio-economic ladder. They reminded themselves of the old maxim that it is better to be envied than to be pitied.

For the most part, the negativity directed by the old-timers toward the newcomers was mean-spirited pettiness. On occasion, however, their behavior could cross beyond the pale of civility. When swastikas were found one morning daubed on public buildings, many old-timers blamed the "greeners" for provoking the gentiles with their foreignness.

The frosty reception extended to my family by some of those fortunate enough to have arrived in Canada before them was at least to some extent a matter of language and culture. Almost all of the old-timers were Jews of Polish origin. The non-Yiddish-speaking Hungarians could not communicate effectively with them, and this proved to be a barrier to their integration, just as it had been in Grugliasco and before that in Auschwitz.

There was another reason for the inhospitable attitude of the old-timers toward the newcomers: the tragedy of the Jews in Europe stood as a yawning chasm between the two groups. Once, in the early years, a neighbor asked my mother, in the course of casual conversation, where she had been during the War. My mother responded matter-of-factly that she was at home in Hungary until the Germans herded her family and all the other Jews of the region into a ghetto, from which they were transported to the Auschwitz concentration camp, where almost all of them were killed. An awkward silence was followed by a deep sigh and a plaintive lament: "You can't imagine how hard life was in Toronto during the Great Depression. And during the War? *Oy!* People didn't even have butter to put on their bread!"

My mother changed the subject. How could she possibly get this woman to understand, when she herself still had difficulty coming to terms with what had happened to her family? Indeed, as the years passed and life became increasingly mundane, she sometimes wondered if it had all just been a delirious nightmare. My mother decided to keep her story to herself.

Slowly, tentatively, the newcomers gained acceptance, as they proved their ability to support themselves, learned to speak English, and became increasingly involved in the community. But several decades would pass before my mother was ready to tell people about her wartime experiences, and until they in turn were ready, even occasionally eager, to listen.

The first summer after arriving in Toronto, my parents packed a picnic basket on a bright, warm Sunday, and went to Sunnyside, a popular recreational area on the shore of Lake Ontario. As they strolled along the boardwalk, they were startled to see two familiar faces coming toward them. Rosita and Ante were among the Croatian couples that had melted in with the Jews in Grugliasco. Rosita had worked for a brief period with my mother in the camp's clothing distribution depot, and they had gotten along well. Glad to recognize someone among all the strangers in Toronto, my parents greeted the couple genially. Ante's face went white as a ghost. He grabbed Rosita's arm, swung around, and walked quickly away without saying a word.

Some people came to the New World and succeeded in banishing the demons of their old life. Others were to be haunted for the rest of their days, no matter how far they ran.

Furs and Mortar

Within a week of arriving in Toronto, the men in the family became fur workers as required by their contracts with the Canadian government. They knew next to nothing about furs, but after years of idleness and insecurity, they were grateful to be gainfully employed, and eager to learn the trade. The Canadian Overseas Fur Commission directed each of them to a different shop in the Spadina garment district. Sanyi was assigned to be a cutter at the National Fur Company and Dezso became a machine operator at the Eastern Fur Company. My father was sent to be a finisher at a small shop whose name he has expelled from his memory. The group decided that my mother would stay at home, doing piecework for a garment manufacturer. This way, she would also be able to baby-sit for Annie and me, while Vera and Kicsi commuted to their jobs at the Melody Dress Company.

Most of the furriers in Toronto were Jewish, but this did not necessarily assure their new employees a congenial work experience. The Ukrainian foreman at my father's first job made it clear from the outset that he detested Jews. He ordered the new worker to walk barefooted into a conditioning vat filled with furs and harsh chemicals. The idea was to jump up and down until the furs were thoroughly permeated by the chemicals. My father suffered a severe reaction in which a fiery rash erupted all over his body and his eyes became red and swollen. He pleaded to be switched to any other job in the shop. The foreman refused the request, cursing all the lazy, blood-sucking Jews unwilling to work for a living.

After several days of this, my mother could no longer bear to see her husband suffering. She arranged for a neighbor to keep an eye on the

66

babies and rode the streetcar to the Canadian Overseas Fur Commission offices at 150 Beverley Street. There, she demanded to see Mr. Daniel Drutz, who was responsible for the refugees' employment assignments. She told Mr. Drutz that she had not come to Canada to see her husband mistreated by a Jew-hater; for that, she could have stayed in Europe. She asked that her husband be reassigned to another shop. Mr. Drutz responded that since she was an incomparably more experienced seamstress than her husband was a fur worker, perhaps it would make better sense for her to go out to work, and have her husband stay home with the little ones. My mother was outraged by this suggestion. Where she came from, the men were responsible for supporting their families, and the women stayed home to care for the household.

In truth, there was more involved than what she told Mr. Drutz. It was not as if my mother was averse to work: the very fact that she was alive was a result of her industriousness. She could never forget her father's parting admonition, just before they were separated at the Auschwitz train station: "Whenever the Germans call for volunteers, Judit, you be the first to step forward." Others thought it clever to conserve their energy by working as little as possible. Eliahu Schwarcz understood that the Germans would regard unproductive Jews as expendable.

Later, in Grugliasco, my mother welcomed the opportunity to work for ORT. She knew it would benefit her and help restore her dignity. Even without remuneration, being engaged in useful activity would be far better than sitting around and feeling sorry for herself. In Canada, she was prepared to sew at home to supplement her husband's income for as long as necessary. But first and foremost, she was determined to be a good mother to her infant son. Who could have imagined, a few years earlier in Auschwitz, that one day she would experience the wondrous joy of having a child of her own? There was not a shred of doubt in her mind; her place was at home raising her son.

When he saw this woman's steely determination, Mr. Drutz relented. He called Max Federman, the president of the Toronto Fur Workers' Union and one of those who had interviewed my father in Rome, and explained the situation. The next day, my father was notified that he was being reassigned to another fur shop.

With renewed vigor, my father started work Monday morning and progressed nicely through the week. On Friday afternoon, he told his new Jewish boss that he could not come to work the next day because he was *shoimer Shabbos*, Sabbath observant. The indignant response was that here, in Canada, people worked six days a week and rested on Sunday, and that any worker who failed to show up Saturday morning for other than documented medical reasons should consider himself fired.

My father was never one to indulge in theological ruminations: he was always a pragmatically-minded man of action, with a keen sense of what works best. His intuition told him that the most effective way to cope with his inner turmoil, to impose order on his chaotic life and infuse it with meaning, was to ground himself in the values that connected him to his stable and happy past. This meant, among other things, observing *Shabbos*. At a time when he was at the mercy of strangers for his economic well being, this proved to be a serious sacrifice. Moreover, it was not as if he won admiration from his fellow Jews for his courageous decision; on the contrary, he provoked scorn and resentment, especially from the formerly observant who felt he was making them look bad.

Predictably, my father's new job at yet another Jewish-owned fur shop only lasted until the first Friday afternoon. He was on the verge of despair when he had the good fortune to be hired by Pulver Furs. Although Mr. Pulver kept his shop open on Saturday like all the others, he was a compassionate gentleman. He allowed his obstinate employee to take the day off, on the understanding that he would have to produce in five days what the others produced in six. My father expressed his gratitude to Mr. Pulver by consistently exceeding the output of his co-workers.

My father's salary in those days was one hundred sixty-two dollars and eighty-nine cents per month. His boss deducted thirty-seven dollars and ninety-two cents to cover the rent on the apartment provided by the Canadian Jewish Congress as part of its commitment to the Canadian government. In the first four months of employment, there was also a payroll deduction of ten percent to cover the sixty-six dollar cost of the two adult train tickets from Halifax to Toronto. The only thing the Rubinsteins received from the Jewish community at no charge was the scrambled egg breakfast at Goldenberg's Restaurant the morning they arrived in Toronto. The Jewish Immigrant Aid Society did offer immigrants a one-hundred dollar loan for the purpose of buying used furniture, repayable at the rate of one dollar per week, but my parents proudly declined to accept the money.

From the beginning, my father was focused on the future. Every month without fail, he set aside twenty-five dollars that went into a special savings account. Never once did he succumb to the temptation to use this money to cover living expenses. The account would continue to grow until there was sufficient capital to fulfill his dream of establishing a business of his own.

Whatever my father had to endure in those early days, Sanyi had a worse problem: it seemed he was not a very good cutter, despite Mrs. Finzi's attempts to teach him. After he mutilated several pelts, his employer fired him. Word got around, and no other furrier was prepared to hire him. Without a job in the fur trade, his immigration status was in jeopardy, but his overriding worry was how he would make a living. In desperation, he decided to become a door-to-door chicken peddler. He would do the pick-ups and deliveries with a battered old bicycle he had found somewhere. Recalling that in the old country the most prized chickens had been the fattest, he picked the plumpest birds from his obliging wholesaler in Kensington Market. But Canadian customers had a leaner taste, and so they declined to buy the chickens. Without refrigeration, the merchandise soon spoiled, and Sanyi's first attempt at entrepreneurship in Canada came to a disastrous end.

Next, he tried sewing neckties out of discarded scraps of fabric, but he knew as much about neckties as he did about chickens. No one was interested in wearing his outlandish creations. After two business failures and with no means of support, Sandor Hofstadter was beginning to despair of succeeding in Canada. At long last, he found a job as a fur coat salesman.

The leaders of the Toronto Jewish community devoted much time and energy to worrying about how they would get their money back from the immigrants.[1] They also kept track of them to make sure they adhered to the terms of their work contracts, so as not to antagonize the authorities. There is no evidence, however, that they maintained contact simply to ensure the newcomers' successful integration in Canada. The records indicate that there were spirited discussions in which a minority among the leadership felt it was unseemly to ask these people to repay everything, after all they had been through. In the end, however, the repayment policy was rationalized as being in the immigrants' best interests. The Canadian

69

Jewish Congress Regional Executive concluded that "unless such commitments were undertaken by the D.P.'s (Displaced Persons), they would be subjected to the same pauperized existence which they had been carrying on in D.P. camps. It needed to be stressed that repayments were being requested in the interests of re-establishing immigrants."[2]

The leaders also seemed to be at least mildly troubled by the contempt shown the newcomers by the old-timers. For example, the minutes of a meeting of the directors of the Jewish Immigrant Aid Society record the following: "It was suggested at the meeting that all future reference to new arrivals be to 'New Canadians' rather than 'D.P.'s', which the immigrants feel is slightly slanderous."[3] Despite this commendable suggestion, key officials continued to use the pejorative term even in written communications, except, of course, those directed to the New Canadians themselves. No one went so far as to suggest dropping the derogatory and contemptuous "*greener*," which cut deeply into the newcomers every time they heard it.

In a radio broadcast explaining to the Toronto public why it was so important to help the immigrants, an unidentified Jewish community leader quoted a typical complaint in those days: "Why are we going out of our way to do all this for the refugees who have been coming to our community? Why do we make such a fuss about seeing that they are provided housing, jobs, medical attention, and financial help? Did anybody provide *me* with this help when I arrived here years ago?"[4]

The leaders were clearly compassionate individuals who wanted to help their distressed fellow Jews from Europe, and went to considerable lengths to do so. But this does not mean that they, or the community they represented, were prepared to accept the survivors as equals once they arrived in Canada. There was really nothing surprising about this, as snobbism towards immigrants is a common phenomenon deeply rooted in human nature. It is interesting to note, however, that even the most prominent and successful members of the Toronto Jewish community tended to be of humble origin, their families having immigrated to Canada years before primarily to escape grinding poverty back home. It is ironic that they should have felt superior to the newcomers, who mostly came from more affluent and cultivated backgrounds than they did: had Hitler not come along to turn their lives inside out, these people would have been perfectly content to remain in the lands of their birth.

The one-year commitment to work in Canada as furriers ended soon enough. The authorities no doubt assumed that once a worker, always a worker, and in the majority of cases, they would have been correct. However, it was simply inconceivable to the entrepreneurially-minded men in my family that they might work for someone else any longer than necessary. On October 7, 1949, each of them received a Department of Labor certificate confirming that he had discharged his undertaking to the Government of Canada to remain in specified employment for a period of twelve months.

The men were determined to become independent businessmen once again, as they had been in Hungary. When the opportunity presented itself, it came from an unexpected quarter. There was in Toronto a furrier by the name of Sholom Goodman, whom the men had met at the Markham Street synagogue. Mr. Goodman had a large, fully equipped shop at Queen and Spadina, but he was nearly bankrupt and struggling along with a single employee. He told the men that they were welcome to set up their own business in a corner of the shop, store their supplies there, and use the machinery as they wished. When they asked Mr. Goodman how much he expected them to pay, he responded that there would be no charge. He simply wanted to help them get established in Canada.

Mr. Goodman lived up to his name. His motivation was pure, but as it turned out, he was to be rewarded for his kindness. In addition to letting the immigrants use his facilities for free, he referred them to his former customers who were reluctant to deal with him because of his financial difficulties. When the men succeeded in securing orders from these customers, they subcontracted the work to Mr. Goodman. He was glad to give his unofficial tenants a wholesale price, and they were glad to pay him in cash.

At the same time, the men were able to build up valuable contacts, create a base of operations, and accumulate capital. Béla and Dezso prudently continued to work full-time at their jobs as fur workers. Sanyi proved not very successful in his latest job as a fur salesman. Thus, he was free to focus his energies on the nascent enterprise in the corner of Mr. Goodman's shop. Before long, the three men were satisfied that they had already learned enough about the fur trade and had amassed sufficient financial resources to establish their own shop. The Rubinstein Fur Company opened for business in a tiny second-storey space at Dundas and Spadina, in the heart of Toronto's garment district.

The partners hurled themselves unreservedly into the new business. Although it placed them at a commercial disadvantage, the shop was closed on Saturdays. No matter how busy things might get on Friday, the door was locked before sundown and everyone went home. But the moment three stars appeared in the sky Saturday night, signaling the end of *Shabbos*, the three men were back at work. Every other day of the week, they were on the go from early in the morning until late at night.

The situation was not a happy one for a sensitive little boy sorely in need of paternal contact. I barely saw my father during those intense years. On weekdays, he was gone in the morning before I awoke, and he returned home long after I was put to bed. On *Shabbos* afternoons, when other fathers were catching up with their children on the week just passed, mine fell into an exhausted slumber and stored up his energy for the week ahead.

My mother tried her best to be both parents to me. One of my earliest and most vivid childhood memories is of sitting on the floor next to her sewing machine. The radio was always on, usually tuned to classical music. I drew with crayons on the scraps of black canvas-like material left over from the fur coat linings my mother had started sewing at home. I then tied the scraps together end to end, forming a long "choo-choo train." I recall with amusement the time I tied the "engine" to my mother's dress as she sat working at her machine. When she stood up and walked away, she was rather surprised to realize she was hauling a "choo-choo train" behind her.

The three partners in the Rubinstein Fur Company soon discovered that the main challenge was not producing fur coats, which they had learned to do well enough. The difficult part was selling them. Not many customers walked up the dingy staircase at 227 Spadina Avenue of their own accord. The new businessmen found themselves at a distinct disadvantage to the established furriers, who had cultivated a customer base over many years and were fluent in English. They arrived at the conclusion that a more proactive sales strategy was required. Sanyi, the youngest of the three, took some driving lessons and got his license, after which they bought their first automobile, an old black jalopy. Every Sunday, Sanyi and Dezso loaded up the car with coats, mostly in large sizes, and drove to the Niagara region, where there were many fruit farmers of Hungarian origin. Using their common mother tongue to establish a rapport, they tried to sweet-talk the stout and dowdy wives of the farmers into buying a fine-looking fur coat. On occasion, the strategy worked.

Late one Sunday night in April of 1953, as Sanyi and Dezso returned to Toronto from a particularly unsuccessful Niagara sales expedition, they were rammed from behind on Lakeshore Boulevard. When they got out to check the damage, the occupants of the other car held them up at gunpoint, quickly transferred all the furs to their own vehicle, and sped off. Unfortunately, the merchandise was not insured.

The partners were deeply shaken by the experience. Vera, who was in the last month of her pregnancy, was so agitated by the news that she went into early labor and gave birth to her daughter, Susie.

The three men had demonstrated a willingness to work very hard and to take risks. However, the fur business yielded very modest profits for all the effort. Now, it was proving to be dangerous as well. Five years after arriving in Toronto, the Rubinstein and Hofstadter families had reached a turning point: they were ready to take on a new challenge.

In the years following the end of the Second World War, housing was in critically short supply in Toronto. The Canadian government's increasingly open immigration policy, combined with the dramatic economic expansion of the post-war era, led to rapid growth in the city's population. The local construction industry simply could not keep up with the explosion in demand for living space.

My parents first encountered this problem the day they arrived in Toronto and found themselves living in a squalid hovel. The search for a better place to live was a constant preoccupation for them, as it was for countless other immigrants. In their first four years in Canada, my parents lived in five different homes in the downtown area. Each was somewhat better than the one before, but all were far from ideal.

The fourth of these homes was on Dundas Street, directly above the jewelry store owned by Wili Bacsi, who had years earlier introduced my parents. Once again, my mother was living under the same roof as her uncle, but this time in far-off Canada. Wili Bacsi had arrived in Toronto in 1950 with his new wife, whom we called Elsa Mama. He was able to bring some money with him from Hungary, and he used it to establish a business. He named his store "Hope's Jewelers," in the *hope*, perhaps, that his Anglicization of "Hofstadter" would appeal to the jewelry-buying public.

It had been a very long time since Wili Bacsi last lived in proximity to small children, and he was not in the best of health, which made him irritable. Whenever I toddled around on the bare kitchen floor above his dining room, he complained to my mother about the racket I was making. As they were not prepared to tie me down to my bed, my parents went searching yet again for a more suitable place to live.

Our last home in the downtown area was a creaky old two-storey house on Hepbourne Street. Despite previous cautionary experience living with relatives, we shared the house with my Uncle Dezso, Aunt Vera, and Annie. They lived on the ground floor and we lived upstairs. Both families agreed early on that the situation was intolerable. Annie was a cute pixie half my size, but that did not prevent her from constantly hitting me and scratching my face with her very sharp nails. This caused a strain on the adults, and they started getting on each other's nerves. For many years, they had all been deprived of privacy in the forced labor, concentration, and refugee camps to which they had been consigned. More than anything else, they needed tranquil personal space where they could reconnect with their inner selves. The business-minded men were also unhappy to be wasting their hard-earned money on rent, with nothing to show for it in the end. My father and uncle concluded that they needed to purchase two separate houses. The problem was, there was simply nothing to buy downtown within their limited means.

Toronto was just beginning to expand northward into the wilderness beyond Eglinton, in response to the insatiable demand for new housing. It was possible to buy a brand-new home north of Wilson Avenue, far from the city, for much less money than something older and smaller downtown. After examining several options, the Rubinstein brothers decided to buy two adjacent bungalows on Vinci Crescent from a well-established local builder. The chief attraction was the cost – fourteen-thousand dollars per house – a substantial sum of money back then, but significantly less than the price of anything comparable downtown. The salesman told them that they each only needed to come up with two-thousand eight-hundred dollars in cash, and the rest would be covered by a long-term mortgage from the Central Mortgage and Housing Corporation. All they had to do was fill out the application forms, which would be submitted on their behalf by the builder. There was just one minor obstacle to overcome: neither my father nor my uncle met the minimum income requirement that would assure their ability to keep up mortgage payments. After a brief struggle with their consciences, they decided to inflate their statements of earnings. Fortunately, the CMHC people were lax in their due diligence and approved the mortgages. The houses were theirs!

Back then, Vinci Crescent was considered to be at the end of the world. It was very far from everything – work, school, stores, and the few people in Toronto the Rubinsteins knew. The nearest bus stop was fifteen minutes away by foot, at the intersection of Bathurst and Wilson. Only once an hour did a bus pull up to the desolate stop, turn around, and flee back to civilization. The entire street shared a single telephone mounted on a pole by the side of the open-ditched dirt road. Whoever happened to be nearest when the phone rang picked it up and went running down the road in search of the person being called. The expectation was that sooner or later, the favor would be returned. The houses were built in a crescent along one side of the road. On the other side were a field of wild raspberry bushes and a pond leaping with frogs.

When they completed the purchase documents for their new homes, the Rubinstein brothers noticed that the builder signed his name with an "X." They were amazed to realize that this man who was able to build an entire street of houses was illiterate. They decided that if someone like him could do it, so could they. Just as they had earlier learned to be furriers, they would now learn to be builders.

They discussed the idea with Sanyi, who continued to live downtown, and the three of them decided to proceed, albeit cautiously. After several years of working hard in Canada, they had something to lose, and they bore responsibilities toward their families. Béla and Dezso continued to run the fur shop, which provided the three families with a livelihood, while Sanyi set out to establish the new venture. Wili Bacsi was willing to be an investor.

It was not an easy decision to make. The three partners appreciated the fact that building a house was far more complicated than sewing a fur coat, and no one was giving them any encouragement. An old-timer in the community lucky enough to have inherited a family business took it upon himself to serve as the newcomers' advisor. He strongly cautioned them against entering the field of construction. Such a foolhardy move, he predicted, could only lead to economic catastrophe. It is always best to stick with what you already know.

In retrospect, the partners clearly made the right decision, but it was far from obvious at the time. *How did they gather the resolve for such a brazen leap in the dark when they still barely spoke English, had no professional training or experience in construction, and no credit at the bank?*

Part of the answer is that these were survivors who had prevailed in far more discouraging situations. They were conditioned by their experience to think positively. Having once started anew after losing everything, they were prepared to do it again, in the hope that this time it would be for good.

Beyond this, the men were driven by something that transcended simple ambition and the desire to establish a better life for themselves and their families. After being subjected to the basest degradation, they were now striving to reassert their humanity by seeking a higher purpose in everything they did. They were driven by an unarticulated need to set things right, to prove that good could in fact prevail against evil. They had already made a promising start by getting married and bringing Jewish children into the world. Now they would continue along the path by achieving success and security.

Having experienced firsthand the frustrations of finding decent and affordable homes for their families, they were well aware of the enormous demand for new housing in Toronto. This demand was clearly not being met by the existing construction industry. The established builders in Toronto at the time were mostly of old English stock, often into the third or even fourth generation of a family business. They knew how to build, but they lacked vision and ambition. As the typical builder saw it, a construction company could build four houses a year. *Why four, and not five or more?* Quite simply, this was the number of houses his father had built in a year, and his grandfather before him. Besides, a family could live very well on the profits generated by four houses, so why bother building any more?

There was a huge void in the Toronto housing industry begging to be filled. During the years of the post-war boom, Jews established a remarkable presence in this industry, largely eclipsing the old English-Canadian builders who had preceded them. There were two basic categories of Jewish builders. Those who had been born and raised in Toronto enjoyed the significant advantages of money, credit, connections, and language skills, and were able to rise quickly to a dominant position. Those who arrived after the War from Europe had very few, if any, of these advantages, and had to struggle much longer and harder to establish themselves. What many of the newcomers did have was a burning desire to succeed, and this went a long way toward compensating for what they lacked.

Of necessity, the partners had learned to be furriers by working for others, as contractually required by the Canadian government. The consequences of any mistakes they may have committed along the way were absorbed by their employers. When they became independent businessmen, however, there was no such learning curve. They scraped together the money to buy an empty lot, and proceeded to build their first house. Their sole employee was Kurti Bacsi, a peasant from Szentistvan who had found his way to Toronto. (In Hungary, any male of a certain age was called "Uncle".) He convinced his compatriots that he was a master builder, citing his experience years earlier helping erect the steeple on the village church.

Unfortunately, Kurti Bacsi had no real knowledge of construction, and he drank heavily on the job. The first house turned out disastrously. The floors and walls were off level, the windows rattled in their frames, and the basement flooded every time it rained. But the demand in Toronto for new homes was so intense that the upstart builders with the shoddy merchandise had no difficulty finding a customer. Needless to say, their first customer was not a happy one. There were a great many follow-up visits to remedy deficiencies, which eroded what was supposed to be the profit. Nevertheless, the first experience provided a wonderful education in how *not* to build a house. By the time they completed their second project, the aspiring builders were starting to understand the fundamentals of construction, and the third house was actually of acceptable quality.

In 1953, when they were confident that they could make at least as good a living in the construction business as they had made in the fur business, the three partners sold the Rubinstein Fur Company. Béla and Dezso joined Sanyi on a full-time basis in the new enterprise.

When the furriers transformed themselves into builders, they began to be known by the Anglicized names "Bill," "Danny," and "Sandy." Along with their steadily improving English, the name-change signaled a growing level of comfort with their new national identity. Little by little, they were becoming Canadians.

Before long, they were sufficiently confident in their house-building skills that they decided to build new homes for their own families. They purchased four undeveloped lots, sitting in a row on Yeoman's Road, one for each family plus one for Wili Bacsi and Elsa Mama. No fences were erected between the houses, so that there was an enormous combined backyard for the children and their friends to play in.

The newly established construction company's first office was a room in the basement of Sandy's house, staffed by a single bookkeeper/secretary. As they had done in the fur business, the new builders devoted themselves single-mindedly to the challenge at hand. No one kept track of hours worked: everyone simply did whatever they could and whatever needed to be done. A rational division of responsibility evolved. Sandy, as the youngest of the group with the best command of English, played the role of "outside" man, assuming responsibility for dealing with the bankers, municipal authorities, and politicians. After all of his disastrous experiences trying to make a living in Toronto, he had finally found his true calling. Clearly, Sandy Hofstedter was not meant to be a fur cutter, chicken peddler, or tie maker: this man was born to be a real estate developer. Danny became the trades and suppliers negotiator and the construction supervisor. He always had a pair of work boots and a hardhat at the ready in the trunk of his car, and he thrived on the rough-and-tumble action of a construction site. My father, as the oldest of the three, played the role of "inside" man, staying in the office and dealing with administrative matters.

The burgeoning metropolis of Toronto had an insatiable appetite for new rental apartments to house its rapidly growing population. In view of the ready availability of serviced land, reasonable construction costs, and easy financing, the partners recognized that this huge demand generated a particularly attractive business opportunity. They decided to switch from single-family houses to small apartment buildings. In swift succession, they built several such structures, which were snapped up by eager purchasers. Intrigued by the vigorous demand among investors for their product, they soon learned that by leaving in a relatively small amount of their own money and securing a low-interest, long-term mortgage, they could become landlords themselves. In this way, they could continue making money indefinitely into the future, with the prospect of eventually paying off the mortgages and owning the buildings outright. From that point on, the partners no longer sold the apartment buildings they completed.

They were eager to build as many of them as possible, but they did not have enough money of their own to provide the necessary equity qualifying them to take out more than a small number of mortgages. Therefore, they entered into a variety of joint ventures with people who were impressed by their ever-growing reputation for quality, integrity, and business acumen.

When they decided to keep the very first apartment building as an investment, the partners realized that someone would have to look after it. Staff had to be hired, rents had to be collected, and bills had to be paid. It was decided that my father would be responsible for this new branch of the business. Within a few years, the company's portfolio of rental apartment buildings expanded dramatically, as it progressed from small, isolated buildings to towering high-rise complexes. In tandem with all this growth, the property management operation grew quickly. Starting from a position of total inexperience, my father learned by trial and error to become an expert property manager. In time, each of the partners became a consummate professional in his designated area of responsibility.

The booming rental apartment industry came crashing to a halt in 1975, when the government of Ontario decided for reasons of political expediency to impose rent controls. Such blatant disregard for private property rights left a very bad taste with my father, reminiscent as it was of the Hungarian Communist government's confiscation of his family's flourmill in Szentistvan three decades earlier. He and his partners resolved not to build any more rental apartments in Ontario.

In retrospect, rent control proved to be a blessing in disguise, since it led to a healthy diversification of the group's real estate activities. H&R Developments, as the company logically if unimaginatively came to be called, did continue to build high-rise residential buildings, both downtown and in the suburbs, but these were sold as condominiums rather than being held as income-producing properties. H&R also became heavily involved in suburban land development projects, eventually building many new communities of single-family homes.

In a dramatic expansion beyond its well-established residential proficiency, the company started in the mid-seventies to develop office and industrial buildings on a substantial scale. These new sectors soon attained a dominant position in the company's activities.

Kurti Bacsi's legendary first house is by now a distant and amusing memory.

To the older members of my family, the freedom to possess land and buildings was a metaphor for solidity and rootedness, the most fitting of antidotes to all the instability and insecurity they had experienced in their lives. Because they were so determined to succeed, the founders were prepared to take significant risks. But once they reached their comfort level, they understood that they had a great deal to lose. The most important thing at that stage was to protect the assets so painstakingly acquired. In retrospect, it is clear that the strategy of slow and steady growth was successful. Some other developers continued to take large business risks long after doing so ceased to be prudent. This enabled them to grow at a prodigious rate during good times, but caused them severe financial distress when the economy inevitably took a downturn.

In light of my family's sojourn in Italy before immigrating to Canada, an interesting dynamic developed in relation to the company's construction workers. The economic crisis that had gripped Italy after the War resulted in widespread unemployment, compelling many of its citizens to seek work opportunities in more prosperous lands. In the early fifties, Canada took in a large number of immigrants from Italy, primarily working-class people from the south of the country. The great Toronto construction boom was under way, and there was a critical shortage of manpower. Local builders, including the Jewish ones, were only too happy to hire Italians to do the work.

It did not take long, however, for certain socio-economic tensions to surface. Some of the Italian workers, realizing that their Jewish employers were making far more money than they were, became jealous and resentful. One such individual told my father that growing up in Italy, he had never thought ill of the Jews, but when he came to Canada and realized that the Jewish builders were growing wealthy while he and his friends were doing all the hard work, he concluded that the anti-Semites had been right after all about the "money-grubbing Jews."

Some things never change. Whatever their origins, people will be people.

A People Like All Others

I retain a vivid memory of the first wedding I ever attended, at the age of four. Vera Néni's younger brother, Bandi, married Magda, a fellow Hungarian immigrant. As the only children at the wedding, Annie and I stood out. It was so exciting to stay up with the grownups long past our bedtime. While the adults were having dinner, Annie and I pranced about on the dance-floor. I distinctly recall that all eyes were on us, doting on every gauche, juvenile movement. When we tired of performing, the audience expressed its appreciation with a sustained round of applause. Everyone in the room regarded children as a treasure to be cherished. Annie and I represented the collective hope for a better future.

My sister Rochelle was born in 1953, shortly after we moved to Vinci Crescent, and I remember how excited I was at the news. I was so proud to tell everyone about my new baby sister, with her cute round face, rosy cheeks, and straw-blond hair.

Though Rochelle and I had the same parents, we developed into very different individuals. Her childhood experiences, after all, were dramatically unlike my own. By the time Rochelle was born, our family was far more secure financially. She had real toys to play with, as opposed to pots and pans and dressmaking remnants. Less than five years after arriving in Canada, our family had its own little bungalow in the suburbs, and was beginning to develop a sense of community with the neighbors. I had started going to school, and English was already the primary language used at home. Rochelle was barely exposed to Hungarian; for her, it was

81

a remote, alien tongue. Whereas I had only one cousin my age, she had several. Unlike her big brother, Rochelle was a Canadian kid.

Having spent my first years as an only child, I was thrilled to have a younger sibling for whom I could serve as a mentor. I loved teaching my little sister whatever I knew. My early efforts scribbling on scraps of fabric next to the sewing machine progressed to drawing on paper with crayons. Rochelle, naturally, wanted to be an "artist" just like her big brother, and I was glad to teach her (though it did not take the talented student very long to surpass her instructor.)

Rochelle's birth had a significant impact upon our parents as well. Having a child born in Canada made them more grounded in their new country. And the opportunity to name their daughter *Rachel Rivka,* in memory of their mothers who had both perished in Auschwitz, completed the commemorative process which began when they named me *Eliahu Mordechai* after their fathers.

It was not until June 29, 1954, however, nearly six years after they arrived in Canada, that my parents were granted Canadian citizenship. For deracinated refugees, the security and stability associated with being once again citizens of a state represented a critical milestone on the path to normalization. Having forfeited their Hungarian citizenship by leaving Hungary illegally after the War, my parents had been stateless for quite a long time.

I was six years old when I was naturalized together with my parents. People familiar with the North American model have often assumed that I automatically acquired Italian citizenship by virtue of being born in Italy. But such was not the case for any of the thousands of postwar babies born to "displaced persons." Like our parents, we were classified by the authorities as "stateless." While civilly if involuntarily hosted by the vanquished Italians, by no means were we welcome to remain permanently in what was at the time an economically distressed country.

With the move to the suburbs, my parents began breaking out of the constraints that had suffocated them downtown. Most of those who had migrated northward were also postwar arrivals from Europe. They had all left the congested and prohibitively expensive city out of the same desire to find housing of an acceptable standard for their growing families. An altogether unexpected benefit of moving to the "wilderness" was that, this time, they did not arrive to an established social order consisting of old-timers at the top and newcomers at the bottom. Ironically, those who had been *greeners* downtown became founding fathers by default when they moved to the suburbs. Because there was no existing hierarchy in the new neighborhoods, merit trumped length of domicile as a determinant of social status, to the advantage of the immigrants. Over the next few decades, virtually the entire Jewish community of Toronto surged northward up Bathurst Street in a re-markable shift of population. Those who had ignored the newcomers when they showed up at *shul* downtown now found themselves being welcomed to the new suburban *shuls* by the very same people they had once snubbed.

The first regular Orthodox services in the new community took place at the back of the only kosher butcher shop in the area. In this frontier set-ting, no one cared where anyone else came from: Each male over the age of thirteen who helped form the *minyan,* the required quorum of ten, was welcome. Additionally, as there was no rabbi or cantor, those who had grown up in Europe with a strong connection to Jewish ritual were able to help lead the services. With the steady and rapid growth of the Jewish population in the area, the burgeoning congregation kept moving to ever-larger premises. Before long, the region's first permanent Orthodox place of worship, the Shaarei Tefillah Synagogue, was established. Those who lived a little further out, like my parents, eventually built the second – Clanton Park Synagogue.

This new *shul* became the focal point of my parents' growing social-ization within the Jewish community. Many of the founders of Clanton Park were postwar arrivals like themselves, and the native-born Canadi-ans in the group enjoyed no privileged status. This did wonders for the newcomers' self-confidence. They began to assume positions of leader-ship, generally quietly and behind the scenes. They prudently conceded the executive positions to those who were able to speak proper English.

My mother continued her scrupulous devotion to *taharas hamish-pachah,* the traditional laws of family purity, which she had begun to ob-serve after her marriage to my father in Grugliasco. For the first few years after moving to the suburbs, she had to travel all the way downtown to find a *mikvah,* a ritual bath. This involved a long walk to the nearest bus stop, three rides on busses, and one on a streetcar. By the time she returned home to Vinci Crescent, it was very late at night. The experience was par-ticularly unpleasant during the winter months, when her still-damp hair would often freeze stiff. All things considered, going to the *mikvah* was less onerous and time-consuming in Canada than it had been in Italy. What remained the same was the aching solitude of the experience: hardly anyone in Toronto observed *taharas hamishpachah* in those days. My mother's resolute determination to continue was sustained by the memory of her own mother faithfully going to the *mikvah* every month until she was deported to Auschwitz along with the other Jews of Szerencs.

As my father's economic standing improved, he was able to relocate his family to ever larger and more comfortable houses. Finally, my parents found the home of their dreams, backing onto an idyllic, heavily-treed ravine, on Timberlane Drive. They were never to move again, and they appreciated their newfound rootedness as a great blessing after so many years of wandering.

One of their neighbors on the street was Morris Starkman. He was the son of Abraham Starkman, who had been the first Toronto resident to welcome my father and uncle into his home, the *Shabbos* after their arrival. One year, Abraham's wife suddenly took ill and was taken to the hospital just before Passover. My parents were pleased to invite Mr. Starkman as their honored guest for the holiday, finally reciprocating his hospitality of long ago.

Mrs. Lerner, the empathetic grocery-selling widow who lived across the street from the Rubinsteins' first home in Toronto, was another acquaintance from the early days who came back into our family's life after many years. She had moved into a seniors' residence nearby, and my mother visited her with devoted regularity. By now very old and in poor health, Mrs. Lerner always received my mother affectionately, as she had from the beginning, with the greeting *"Vus macht mein greener?"* - How is my greenhorn doing? Each time, my mother would smile and ask how long she would continue to be a *greener*. The invariable response was: *"Mein kind, fur eibig!"* (My child, forever!)

Over the years, my mother had mastered the English language quite effectively. Mrs. Lerner, the virtually life-long Canadian, still spoke only Yiddish.

Canada afforded my parents the opportunity to work hard and attain the basic self-sufficiency of which they had dreamt in Grugliasco.

The degree of prosperity they eventually achieved was far beyond any-thing they had ever dared to imagine. Yet, they never allowed their suc-cess in Canada to go to their heads. As far as they were concerned, they were no better than anyone else, only luckier. No matter how many years they had been living in Canada, they never stopped seeing themselves as survivors, refugees, immigrants. A recurring theme articulated by people who knew my father is admiration for his disarming modesty and lack of presumption. He never played the "boss," never demanded deference from his employees. He would often surprise low-level workers by solicit-ing their advice on a problem. As a one-time workingman, he maintained a healthy respect for the wisdom born of real-life experience.

Although she can permit herself any indulgence she fancies, my mother the seamstress still sews her own clothes on the old sewing ma-chine she keeps in the basement. The few ready-made items that she does buy come from a discount chain store; she has never felt comfortable shopping at upscale establishments. Material things simply hold no al-lure for her. And, although she has always been a striking woman, this is certainly not part of her self-image. In line with this, when evaluating other people, she eschews superficial traits and focuses on character and intelligence.

For many years, my mother had an Italian cleaning lady coming to the house once a week. (In her mind, any greater frequency would be an unwarranted indulgence.) We always knew that there would be fresh bread on Wednesday morning, because Caterina did not eat day-old bread. The leftovers would be popped in the toaster or rendered into croutons or stuffing, but they would never be thrown out. My parents always treated food with great reverence, never forgetting that they had once been deprived of it. They taught me to eat whatever I was served, and to finish everything on my plate. There are many people around the world, they would constantly remind me, who go to bed hungry every night, and it is a special blessing to have enough to eat.

When my parents got married, my father was already an accom-plished cook, while my mother was a novice in the kitchen. Rozsa Schwarcz thought she had plenty of time to teach her daughter basic culinary skills before she married, but the ghetto and the deportations disrupted all manner of well-laid plans. My father, on the other hand, had the best possible teacher in Tera Néni. While waiting in vain for his family to return, he passed the time and calmed his nerves by mastering the classic Hungarian recipes: *gulyás, rákot krumpli, palacsinta, mákos tésta.* My mother learned to cook when she finally had a proper kitchen of her own in Toronto. She certainly made up for lost time, and became an excellent chef as well as an accomplished baker. In later years, her grandchildren's favorite activity was going to Grandma's house to bake cookies or decorate a birthday cake.

Both of my parents grew up in traditional Jewish homes. Szerencs, the mid-sized industrial town where my mother's family lived, had a well-organized and dynamic Jewish community of about nine hundred members. There were no separate Jewish schools in Szerencs, and the Jewish children attended public school. In Hungary, in those days, religious instruction was a mandatory part of the curriculum. For two hours every week, the Christian students went off to their classes and the Jewish students to their own. My maternal grandfather, Eliahu Schwarcz, made his living teaching the fundamentals of Judaism to the Jewish students in one of the public high schools. The majority of Jews in Szerencs were traditionally observant. For them, being Jewish meant preserving the age-old religious practices learned by example at home. Formal Jewish education played a minor role in molding their identity.

In Szentistvan, the Hungarian peasant village where my father lived, Judaism was visceral rather than cerebral. There were only a few Jewish families in Szentistvan, and the opportunities to acquire a Jewish education in such a place were limited. My paternal grandfather, Mordechai Rubinstein, arranged for a *melamed*, a traditional Jewish teacher, to come to the house for several hours each week. The *melamed* taught the children to read, if not necessarily to understand, the *Siddur* and *Chumash*, the Jewish prayer book and the Five Books of Moses. The Rubinstein children developed a strong Jewish consciousness by learning from their parents' personal example how to live a Jewish life and keep a Jewish home.

When they arrived in Canada, my parents faced a number of challenges in adjusting to their new circumstances. Having been torn from their roots, they craved the solace and security of belonging to a Jewish community. They were anxious to return to the kind of Jewish life that they had known in Hungary, but this option simply did not exist in

Toronto. When they went to *shul*, they felt comfortable with the familiar service. But in Canada, membership in an Orthodox synagogue did not generally entail observance of such basics as *Shabbos* and the dietary laws.

Nor could my parents look to their fellow survivors for reassurance. Although the majority had been raised in traditional homes, most had lost their faith. Like my parents, many felt the need to belong to a Jewish community, but they tended to join the rapidly growing Conservative synagogues in the new suburbs, which offered them a sense of belonging without making rigorous religious demands of them.

My parents were determined to provide their children with the best possible schooling. Such emphasis on the importance of education is a virtually universal characteristic of survivors. It goes beyond the long-established Jewish appreciation of education as an effective tool for a weak and oppressed minority in search of a qualitative edge. For survivors, a reverent attitude toward education is rooted in their direct personal experience. How often has the mantra been repeated: "Your enemies can take away all your earthly possessions, but they cannot take away what is stored inside your head."

At the same time, it was very important to my parents that their children develop a strong Jewish identity. They felt a powerful obligation to honor the memory of their own parents by keeping alive those things that had defined them as Jews and passing these on to their children. My parents had decided when I was born that the household they were establishing would resemble those in which they had grown up. They would teach their children to be good Jews by providing a living model at home.

While my parents were preoccupied with making a living and finding their way in the new country, their infant son was growing. Before they realized it, I was old enough to go to school. They knew there were Jewish schools in Toronto, but the very concept was alien to their own experience. To whom could they turn for guidance? Their English was still limited, and they knew hardly anyone in the established Jewish community.

Sholom Goodman, who had been so helpful to my father and his partners when they went into the fur business for themselves, was once again destined to play the role of guiding spirit. My parents knew that after closing his fur shop, Mr. Goodman had become a Jewish studies teacher at the Toronto Hebrew Day School. When they sought his advice, he recommended that they send me to this school, where I would receive an excellent general education preparing me for a successful life in Canada, as well as a first-rate Jewish education linking me to my heritage. Unfamiliar as this concept of a full-service Jewish school was to them, my parents concluded that Mr. Goodman's suggestion was a sound one. In a community where the standard of Jewish observance was so low, one could no longer rely on just the home to foster a strong Jewish identity in children. The rest of the family was not impressed by my parents' extravagant idea: public school, after all, was free, and who needed so much Jewish education? What had been good enough in the old country should be good enough in Canada.

However, my parents held their ground. The tuition would be a financial sacrifice, but somehow they would manage. Although they were advised that they could apply for a subsidy, my parents were too proud to take money from the community. In Grugliasco, they had been humiliated by their dependence on others for the most basic of needs, but they simply had no choice. Now that they were free to work for a living, they were determined to take care of themselves.

Despite their initial reaction, the rest of the family soon came around to my parents' view. Annie followed me to the Toronto Hebrew Day School, and eventually so did all the other children as they reached school age. There was no looking back: with the passing of the years, my family grew ever more committed to the cause of Jewish education, providing both lay leadership and philanthropic support.

By the early sixties, the Jewish day school population in Toronto had grown dramatically. This was largely due to the postwar immigrants. Not only did a disproportionate number of them send their own children to these schools, but as they attained economic security and social acceptance, they also began to exert influence on the character of the schools.

The standard of Jewish commitment had risen enough in the interim that the community was now ready for a continuation of the double curriculum approach at the high school level. Some of my classmates in the graduating class of the Toronto Hebrew Day School continued on as the first class of what would later become the Community Hebrew Academy of Toronto. Others, including me, went to a newly established school that was without precedent in Toronto. The Ner Israel Rabbinical College of Baltimore, Maryland had been invited to establish a yeshiva high school in Toronto, after Yeshiva University of New York declined the opportunity. Those behind the initiative were mostly post-war immigrants, sufficiently self-confident by then to emulate the traditional European educational model. The Jewish studies curriculum in a yeshiva consisted almost entirely of the Talmud and its commentaries. It was not an easy sell: Rabbi Shalom Gold, the founding principal, had to devote a great deal of time and energy to convincing parents like my own that their sons would receive a proper general education qualifying them for university admission.

I have acquired from my parents an appreciation for the moral imperative of transmitting a strong Jewish consciousness to the next generation. However, thanks to them, I have also developed a certain skepticism about the prevailing notion that formal Jewish education is the key to this. Although my parents themselves received almost no such education, their Jewish identity was vigorous. Judaism has been for them intuitive and experiential, inspired directly by the way their own parents lived their lives. Today, those who are unwilling or unable to live the kind of life that has always fostered a strong identification with Judaism tend to place unrealistic expectations upon formal Jewish education as the guarantor of a Jewish future.

It does not require much factual knowledge to live a vibrant Jewish life, and in our increasingly wired world, this knowledge is easy to attain. The real issue is the individual Jew's motivation to seek it out and act on it. Jewish literacy does not, in and of itself, assure Jewish identity. One can acquire an intensive Jewish education through high school; one can even become a university professor of Jewish studies, without necessarily forming an emotional commitment to living a Jewish life. The key to forming such a commitment is actually *doing* the rather simple things one has learned about, and doing them unconditionally. Such observance moves beyond mere nostalgia or folklore, and becomes an integral part of a person's being. An individual whose life encompasses a critical mass of Jewish activity will seek a spouse who wishes to live the same way, and together, they will make sure their children do so as well.

"Do not oppress a stranger; you know the feelings of a stranger, for you were strangers in the Land of Egypt."[1] As a consequence of their own early

experiences as strangers in Toronto, the Rubinsteins developed a special appreciation for this Biblical injunction. Now that they had become more established and laid down roots in the community, they always made sure to look out for those who were "strangers."

When Moroccan Jews began pouring into Toronto in the late sixties, mostly arriving with few possessions, my mother helped organize a campaign to collect used clothing for them. A merchant who had come from Morocco several years earlier offered to store the clothing free of charge in the basement of his shop on Bathurst Street. The offer was accepted with gratitude – until someone discovered that he was picking out the best garments and selling them for his personal profit. My mother was disappointed, but she was not really surprised. She recalled the shameful behavior of some people who had worked with her in the baby-clothing depot in Grugliasco. Instead of distributing the clothes to the parents of newborns, they took the best items for themselves and sold them in the marketplace. My mother remembers being deeply disturbed at the time: How could they do such a thing, after what everyone in the camp had been through so recently?

Years later, when the first wave of Soviet Jews began arriving in Toronto, my parents befriended a young couple, Vladimir and Ludmilla, who had a baby son. Perhaps this family reminded them of their own situation when they first arrived in Toronto. They did everything they could to help the newcomers adjust to their new life. Yet, Vladimir complained incessantly about how difficult it was in Canada, and how people were not prepared to put themselves out for strangers without money. My parents soon concluded that with such a negative attitude, he would never adjust to life in Canada. The friendship cooled, and Vladimir and Ludmilla disappeared.

A positive attitude was one of the main factors enabling my parents to build a successful new life in Canada. They were grateful for the opportunity to live and work in freedom, and beyond this, they expected nothing from anyone. If ever they were tempted by the all-too-human impulse to feel sorry for themselves, they quickly set it aside, realizing that self-pity would be a serious impediment to their rehabilitation.

In the spring of 1958, amid great excitement, my mother and Kicsi Hofstedter embarked on a journey to Israel. It was the first time anyone in the family had left Canada since arriving nine and a half years earlier. Israel was no simple travel destination: for survivors, it was a truly miraculous land, a beacon of hope in a once hopeless world. My mother longed to meet her brother Yitzchak, whom she had last seen in Hungary after the War. Kicsi, for her part, yearned for a reunion with her sisters, Magdi and Borika.

The trip proved to be a major sensation. The entire family went to Malton Airport to bid bon voyage to the world travelers, and when they arrived at Lod Airport in Israel, they were received with great exuberance by the Israeli relatives. When Kicsi and my mother returned to Toronto three weeks later, everyone gathered around to listen to their detailed description of the wonders they had witnessed. *Imagine, a Jewish state with Jewish farmers and Jewish traffic policewomen!* However, the highlight, by all accounts, was the description of the tenth anniversary military parade in Jerusalem on Independence Day. Tears of joy flowed at the very notion of Jewish soldiers, Jewish tanks, and Jewish fighter planes. The family members looked at one another, and knew they were thinking the same thought: what a tragic pity that a Jewish state did not exist during the War, when all the gates were slammed shut and the Jews of Europe were led helplessly to the gas chambers.

The older generation of Israeli relatives exhibited some rather striking characteristics. Unlike their contemporaries in Canada, who always spoke Hungarian among themselves, the Israelis made a point of always speaking Hebrew, and speaking it well. They did this self-consciously and with great determination, aware of their role in the grand experiment in nation building that was modern Israel. The one thing that was able to tie together such a diverse group of people from around the world was a common mastery of the reborn language of the Jews.

They also engaged in passionate and well-informed discussion concerning all facets of their beloved country. The Israeli family members were emotionally engaged with Israel in a way that I could not imagine the Canadian family members being engaged with Canada. The Israelis' sense of enfranchisement and commitment was very appealing compared to the Canadians' appreciative but less emotional relationship with Canada.

Furthermore, there were striking differences with regard to religion between those who ended up in Israel and those who ended up in

Canada. Almost all the Israelis were alienated from traditional Jewish practice. The only exceptions seemed to be a few elderly people who followed in the old ways as a matter of well-trodden habit. They were out of step with their own children and even more so with their Israeli-born grandchildren.

My parents, like many survivors, embraced the classical Zionist view of Israel as a place of refuge for Jews in distress. There is a solemn duty to support Israel and make it strong, so that if another Hitler should ever arise, God forbid, we would have somewhere to go. Wonderful as Canada may be, there are no guarantees of safety even here. We need to keep reminding ourselves that the murder of six million Jews had its origins in Germany, the most civilized of nations.

In addition, my parents never forgot that Israel had been their original destination. Arriving in Canada was an accident. When my parents spoke about the relatives in Israel, it was always with a sense of "there but for fortune," as if to say that things really could have turned out otherwise.

In 1979, my parents traveled to Montevideo, Uruguay to visit their dear old friends, Miklos and Anczi Tenenbaum. They had first met the Tenenbaums in Grugliasco and were immediately drawn to them, as they were among the few fellow Hungarian-speakers in the camp. Aside from this linguistic affinity, Miklos and Anczi were delightful people with personal backgrounds similar to those of my parents. Early in the relationship, they had made a resolution that wherever in the world fate carried them, they would go together. When the Canadian fur-workers delegation arrived in Italy, Miklos traveled to Rome for an interview, but the quota was filled long before he had a chance to plead his case. The Tenenbaums were quite distraught that they could not join the Rubinsteins and Hofstedters on the voyage to Canada. Some time later, the opportunity arose for them to immigrate to Uruguay.

The much-anticipated reunion was emotionally charged: Miklos and Anczi greeted my parents at the Montevideo Airport like long-lost relatives. When they entered the Tenenbaums' home, my parents were surprised to see household effects packed in crates, ready for shipping. Their hosts announced that they were moving to Israel.

What had brought about this dramatic decision? Several weeks earlier, the Tenenbaums had been invited by a wealthy Jewish acquaintance to a lavish party celebrating the completion of his opulent new mansion. The cream of Montevideo society was there, and the liquor flowed freely. A prominent politician got up to propose a toast: "Señor Goldberg, we congratulate you on your beautiful new home. It is truly breathtaking. Just remember – you Jews may own the fancy houses, but we real Uruguayans will always own the land beneath your feet."

Miklos and Anczi were so disturbed they could not sleep that night. They kept asking themselves, had they survived the concentration camps and struggled to rebuild their lives so that it should now come to this? By morning, they had decided to move to Israel.

My mother has often commented on the irony of this story. She was the "lucky" one whose husband made it into the furriers' quota, and so she ended up living her life in Canada instead of Israel, the land of her dreams. The "unlucky" Tenenbaums, who had to settle for Uruguay, were the ones who ultimately ended up in Israel.

For those who share my parents' background, the State of Israel is a powerful symbol of hope for the future. The return of the Jewish people to its ancient homeland makes possible a mending of the broken Jewish spirit and gives Jews a control over their destiny, which had been lacking for two millennia, with frequently tragic consequences. Each survivor who succeeded in putting his life back together after the War saw the same phenomenon being played out on the national level in Israel, and this helped forge a deep identification with the fledgling state.

It must be said, however, that there is another, darker, side. During the Six Day War in 1967, I witnessed my parents hovering on the edge of despair. For the first few days, the only source of news was the Arab media, crowing about the triumphant Arab armies driving the Jews into the sea. The government of Israel wisely kept silent. Only when it was almost over did we learn that the Arabs had been lying, that in reality they had suffered a massive and humiliating defeat at the hands of the Israel Defense Forces.

During those dreadful few days, my parents wondered whether all the years of hard work rebuilding their lives had been for naught. It seemed that those who wished to annihilate the Jewish people were finally succeeding. My parents barely spoke, but their faces betrayed the anguish within. When the war ended, mercifully quickly, and they learned of Israel's great victory, they reacted with indescribable jubilation.

As children of the twentieth century, my parents have lived through an astonishing range of transformative events. Armed conflicts on a previously unimaginable scale raged furiously before they were finally extinguished. Grand ideologies arose and fell amid the deadening despair of failed promises. Discredited empires collapsed only to be replaced by new ones, pregnant with untested promise. As Jews, my parents have lived through what was surely the most eventful period in the *far-too-eventful* history of the Jewish people. Within a few years, they lurched from the emotional low of the destruction of European Jewry to the emotional high of the birth of Israel. It is truly astonishing that they were able to take everything in stride. It has been a very long journey from small-town Hungary to big-city Canada. The changes my parents witnessed and the challenges they overcame along the way boggle the mind. But the most remarkable thing is that they managed to remain true to themselves. Never did they lose their moral compass, even in the darkest days when it appeared that the bulk of humankind had done so. The coexistence of such extraordinary adaptability and dedication to principle within a single individual is rare to find. It is a special privilege to be the child of *two* such individuals and to have had the opportunity to learn from their personal examples.

My parents walked away from their homes in Hungary and never looked back. Later, they left the camp in Italy focused resolutely on the future. When they finally arrived in Canada, they directed all their energies to the challenge of building a new reality. By doing so, they were able to advance far beyond what they left behind. Capitulation to self-pity would certainly have been understandable: if anyone in the world had a legitimate grievance against humankind, it was the Jews who had endured the horrors of Nazi-occupied Europe. Yet, my parents and many others like them remained remarkably free of recrimination or regret. Perhaps this is the key to understanding the astonishing survival of the Jewish people throughout the ages: instead of dwelling on past injustices, Jews have, as a rule, been able to pick up the broken pieces and put them back together with quiet nobility.

My parents have never been judgmental or vindictive. They consistently maintained that each human being is entitled to be evaluated on his individual merit, and not held responsible for the misdeeds of others in his group. In practical terms, my parents' ability to avoid reciprocating the hatred of the haters facilitated their emotional healing. It enabled them to let the negative energy drain out of them, so that all that was left was the positive energy they needed to rebuild their lives.

This does not mean, however, that my parents were naïve regarding the human capacity for evil. It is an unfortunate fact that there have always been, and no doubt always will be, people of ill will ready to cause others harm. My parents knew this all too well from their personal experience. The Nazis tried to dehumanize their victims by destroying their hope for the future. Therefore, we are obligated to cherish this hope and protect it zealously. We do this by reminding ourselves that while some people are undeniably bad, it is also the case that others are good. We stress the point by striving in our own lives to be exemplars of virtuous behavior.

Although my parents achieved significant success in Canada, they remained what they had always been – good-hearted, unassuming, likeable people. They treated everyone with the same respect that they drew to themselves and which they believed was the natural entitlement of all human beings.

Confronting the Past

For a long time, I had wanted to travel to my ancestral homeland. But whenever I raised the subject with my parents, they reacted with dismay. Upon leaving Hungary after the War, they slammed the door hard behind them, vowing never again to set foot in that accursed land. They could not grasp why a child of theirs would want to go to Hungary, of all places in the world. I tried to explain that it was precisely my awareness of their past that drove me: I could not truly know myself until I truly knew them. That required interacting with the milieu that had first nurtured and shaped them, and then roughly cast them out. I would plunge into my family's crucible just once, with a solemn pledge that this would be the end of the matter.

My parents finally yielded to my stubborn determination. The ensuing visit to Hungary in 1972 has remained to this day the most emotionally wrenching experience of my life.

Through a family acquaintance, I arranged to rent a room in the Budapest apartment of an elderly Jewish widow. Budapest was a vibrant and sophisticated city, but I could not relate to it. My parents came from smaller, humbler places. And so, I took the train to Szentistvan.

I arrived unannounced and certainly unexpected. I knew that my father's childhood playmate, the son of the Rubinstein family's housekeeper, was still living in Szentistvan, and that my father corresponded with him and periodically sent him money. I asked the first person I encountered on the main road whether he knew Pista Varga.

"And who, if it may be permitted to ask the honorable gentleman, might be seeking him?" The Hungarian language has an odd formality

96

to it that is particularly charming when it emerges from the mouth of a peasant.

"I am Béla Rubinstein's son from Canada."

Within a few minutes, Pista was there, hugging and kissing me, inquiring about the welfare of his dear old friend Béla. Very quickly, I found myself surrounded by what felt like the entire population of Szentistvan. Stout peasant women with brightly colored headscarves and gleaming gold teeth embraced me. Everyone was chattering excitedly. I was flattered by all the attention. It was disconcerting, however, to hear the villagers referring to me, and to my people, as *a zsidok*, the Jews:

"You know, it's a shame the Jews are gone. They were good people, after all. Things just haven't been the same without them."

"Someone told me that the Germans treated the Jews really terribly when they took them away from here."

"You don't have to feel sorry for the Jews. They are all very clever, and they always know how to take care of themselves."

"Yes, I heard that they all moved to America and became millionaires."

One of the peasant women pressed her weather-beaten face up to mine. The anxious tone of her voice suggested a conscience in search of absolution.

"Tell me, Béla's son, is it really true that all the Jews went to America?"

I was too choked up to answer.

Pista took me to see my father's once handsome home in the center of the village. Having been subdivided into tiny cubicles on the principle of proletarian equality, it now served as a residence for the indigent elderly. The front entrance area facing the road was being used as the village post office. The flourmill behind the house, which had once been a mainstay of the local economy, had long ago been nationalized and presented as a gift to the Hungarian people. It was a gutted, abandoned shambles.

The men decided to treat their special visitor in the time-honored tradition. Off we went to the local tavern, to drink to the health of the Rubinstein family in far-away Canada. Pista ordered a round of *Egri Bikavér*, a popular Hungarian red wine. When the waiter placed the glasses on the table, a long dormant memory kicked in.

"Wait!" exclaimed Pista. "He can't drink that! The Jews only drink their own special wine."

The peasants of Szentistvan wished their friends in Toronto a long and happy life, and downed their *Egri Bikavér* while I had a draught beer. My already strong sense of separateness was further reinforced. These warm, hospitable people who so naturally called me "*a zsido*" unintentionally impressed upon me how out of place I was in the village that had once been my father's home. Now I understood my parents' discomfort about the trip: the Jews of Szentistvan were gone, never to return, and I simply had no business being there.

Before leaving Szentistvan, I asked Pista to take me to the Jewish cemetery. I knew that the only member of the family buried there was my grandfather Mordechai, who had the good fortune to die of natural causes before the Germans deported the others to Auschwitz. The cemetery was overgrown with weeds, and many of the tombstones were in a state of disrepair. Pista remembered where my grandfather was buried, and he led me to the spot. The engraved Hebrew inscription was perfectly legible.

Over the years since then, the old inhibitions have melted away. By now, just about everyone in the family has traveled to Hungary on a pilgrimage to the gravesite of our patriarch, Mordechai the son of Dov and Rivka Rubinstein. Even my parents eventually relented. My mother convinced my father that he had a special obligation to fulfill the *mitzvah* of *kever avos*. To her everlasting sorrow, she had no parental graves to visit, but her husband had this privilege, so rare among people of their circumstances. *How could he not go back, at least once, to honor his father's memory?*

To the end, my father kept in touch with his childhood companion, who, like him, merited exceptional longevity. He sent Pista money every year before Christmas, and in turn, he received a nice Christmas card heaping blessings on the entire Rubinstein family.

I still had a mission to fulfill before leaving Hungary. My father's former brother-in-law, Miklos Farago, was living in Salgotarjan with his wife and two daughters. Years earlier, Miklos had urged my father to find himself a new wife in Hungary before setting out into an uncertain world. This turned out to be excellent advice, and my father felt a debt of gratitude towards him. The Faragos had managed to save their beautiful grand piano and other pieces of fine furniture before the deportation, and were able to reclaim them at the end of the War. The only problem was that the Communist government would not let them remove these possessions from Hungary, and they could not bear to leave them behind. From early on, my father had begged Miklos to come to Canada for the sake of the girls, who had no future as Jews in small-town Hungary. He offered to sponsor their immigration and help with their expenses, although he was still a struggling immigrant himself. Miklos and his wife could simply not let go of the piano, and so they stayed.

When he drove me to the airport for the flight to Hungary, my father asked me to deliver a new message to Miklos.

I took the train to Salgotarjan, a bleak, polluted industrial town in the far north of the country. The Faragos lived in a small apartment in a crumbling Stalin-era building. They welcomed me graciously into their home. There in the middle of the living room stood the beloved piano in all its grandeur. I delivered my father's message to Miklos in the best Hungarian I could muster. The government of Hungary was now prepared to allow a certain number of Jews to immigrate to Israel each year. If the Faragos agreed to go, my father would fully support them, which he was by now in a position to do, for as long as necessary. Miklos grew agitated and blurted out that he could not possibly go to Israel because he was afraid of the constant wars with the Arabs.

It was then I realized that it had not really been about the piano at all.

The girls grew up and married local Hungarian men. Years later, we were intrigued to learn that Beatrice, one of Miklos' granddaughters, had decided to escape the sooty hopelessness of Salgotarjan and move to Israel. She learned to speak Hebrew, renamed herself Efrat, found an Israeli boyfriend, and is proud to be living in the reborn homeland of her people.

The purpose of the trip had been served: I *did* get Hungary out of my system. I succeeded in gaining considerable insight into the country that first embraced and then spurned its Jewish citizens, including my parents, and thus I now have a better grasp of who I am. That was the end of it, just as I had promised. When I encountered the naively candid peasants of Szentistvan, I came the closest I ever could to understanding the old world of my father. After that, it was time to stop looking backward and to start moving forward into my own future.

I have since surmised that the reason my parents were so upset by my decision to go to Hungary was that it seemed to subvert their resolute desire to move ahead in a positive manner, away from the negativity Hungary represented to them. Not everyone is blessed with the kind of courage it takes to break with a bad past and create a better future. Poor Miklos Farago was not so blessed, but one of his granddaughters was. My parents were endowed with an abundance of this quality. When I insisted on returning to that which they had so decisively left behind, they must have been wondering whether they had somehow failed in transmitting their legacy to their son.

Hungary may have been the land where all of my family lived, but Poland was the land where most of my family died. In 1982, Renée and I had the opportunity to travel to this graveyard of the Jewish people. I quite naturally assumed that it would be a powerful emotional experience. For many children of survivors who are deeply touched by their parents' past, a pilgrimage to Auschwitz is *de rigueur*. What better way can there be to understand our parents than to confront the death camp that has become a metaphor for the mass murder of the Jews? In my particular case, the connection to Auschwitz was more than metaphorical, as my mother had been a slave-laborer there and most of my family was killed there. Yet, I had never been preoccupied with Auschwitz as I had been with Hungary. I do not recall that it ever came up as a topic of conversation while Renée and I were dating. Only after we were engaged did we discover that our mothers had both been in Auschwitz at the same time and had each lost parents and siblings there.

My parents took the news of our journey to Poland very calmly. My mother even provided a briefing and drew me a map of the camp from memory. She made a point of marking the area nicknamed "Kanada," where she worked for a time sorting the confiscated possessions of newly arrived Jewish inmates. She was clearly amused by the retrospective irony of the name. Apparently, Canada had been regarded in Auschwitz as a land of plenty where anything and everything could be found.

I remember the dark sense of anticipation Renée and I both felt on the bus ride from Krakow to Auschwitz. I braced myself when I saw the *ARBEIT MACHT FREI* sign over the entrance gate, knowing that this was the first thing my mother and all my murdered relatives saw when they arrived at the camp. I was prepared to be overwhelmed by a rush of emotions.

To my bewilderment, Auschwitz left me cold. I saw the luggage, the eyeglasses, some of the clothing which my mother could very well have helped sort, sitting heaped in grotesque piles behind glass display cases. I saw the remnants of the incompletely destroyed crematoria left behind by the hastily retreating Germans. I even spotted fragments on the ground of what appeared to be human bone, which, for all I knew, came from members of my own family. I felt deeply uncomfortable about the flatness of my response, but it was something beyond my control.

How do I explain such emotional numbness in the death trap of my family and people? Perhaps I was unconsciously mimicking my parents, both of whom learned to deal with the enormity of the tragedy by detaching themselves emotionally from it, each in a very different way, reflecting their individual personalities and temperaments. Their gaze was fixed on that which came after Auschwitz, and they were drawn to those places that pointed optimistically toward the future. As their son, I was interested in Hungary because I thought it connected me to my ruptured past. I was interested in Italy because it represented the spiritual rehabilitation of my family, preparing them for a new life in Canada. Most of all, I was fervently interested in Israel because it embodies Jewish hope for the future. Poland and Auschwitz symbolize death and hopelessness. I refuse to identify with these things, and so I have disengaged myself emotionally from the places that symbolize them.

Over the years, all of my children have made the trip to Poland at least once. I am always intrigued to observe their reactions. Of course, each is a distinct individual, so there are differences among them. But without fail, my children report that it was a deeply moving experience, especially the visit to Auschwitz. None of them ever visited Poland without continuing onward to Israel, which is absolutely crucial. If darkness is not followed by light, the inevitable consequence is despair. A trip to Poland alone could lead a young Jew to the conclusion that to be Jewish in our time means to be despised and persecuted, and perhaps murdered.

If this were so, why would *anyone* want to remain Jewish? Culminating the trip in Israel gives young people a feeling of pride, a healthy sense that *am Yisrael chai,* the people of Israel lives.

Why are my children capable of being moved by Auschwitz while I am not? Perhaps it is because *they* are *my* children, whereas *I* am my parents' child.

The circumstances of my first trip to Torino were altogether different. It was actually my mother's voracious reading that led me to rediscover the place of my birth.

My mother has a deep passion for books. Although her formal education ended with the fourth grade, she has read many more books than most university graduates. She reads primarily in English, a language she first encountered as an adult and never had the opportunity to study properly. She has a particular appetite for memoirs by survivors, devouring everything that comes to her attention in this genre. It is a highly ambivalent enterprise for her: on the one hand, being reminded of her own wartime experiences upsets her, and on the other, reading the stories of other survivors reinforces her strong sense of kinship with this special group, and gives her a feeling of connectedness to her destroyed past.

While attending the Jewish Book Fair in Toronto in November 1993, my mother came across a volume with the title *Smoke Over Birkenau,*[1] written by an Italian Jewish woman named Liana Millu. Reading the book at home, she grew increasingly emotional as she realized that this stranger had been in all the same places in Auschwitz as she had, and at the same times. They were even together on the forced march to Schwerin as the Germans retreated before the Allies. She also learned that the blue number tattooed by the Nazis on Liana Millu's forearm was A-5384. Her own number was A-6876, which meant that Liana arrived at Auschwitz shortly before her, toward the end of May 1944. (I am unable to commit my mother's number to memory, or even to say which arm it is on. I understand this is common among the children of survivors who bear concentration camp tattoos.)

My mother was determined to contact Liana. With the assistance of the Italian Consulate-General in Toronto, she had a home address and phone number in Genova the next day. The meeting of these two strangers over the telephone was very poignant. In Auschwitz, they could not have communicated with one another, because the native of Hungary and the native of Italy lacked a common language. In the years since, both had learned to speak English, and instantly, they were like sisters. They resolved to meet in person, but Liana had grown old and infirm, and was not able to travel. My mother decided she would fly to Italy as soon as possible.

Fortuitously, her opportunity arose in April 1994, when our friends the Netzers invited Renée and me to a *Bar Mitzvah* in Milano. We asked my mother to accompany us on the trip. Without hesitation, she agreed.

A glance at the map showed that the cities of Milano, Genova, and Torino formed a compact triangle linked by modern highways. Our itinerary quickly took shape: we would begin with a visit to Liana Millu in Genova, continue on to the site of the refugee camp in Grugliasco, and end up in Milano for the *Bar Mitzvah*.

As expected, the "reunion" was an emotional event. Liana Millu came from a very old Italian Jewish family. She was highly educated and cultured, and, like most Italian Jews, much more Italian than Jewish. She had never married or raised children, and she was devoted to her career as a university lecturer and writer. In short, Liana had very little in common with my mother, other than her love of books and Auschwitz pedigree. This was all the two women needed to feel a powerful bond. Hours of impassioned conversation were followed by a long and tearful embrace, a resolution to keep in touch, and a reluctant parting.

Over the years, I have often fantasized about visiting the refugee camp where I started my life. No member of the family had ever gone back to Grugliasco after leaving for Canada in 1948. No one had even taken the trouble to make inquiries, and so we had no idea what had become of the camp in the years after we left. I, for one, was very curious to find out. In my mind, Grugliasco was the central icon of my family's post-war rehabilitation: it represented for me the way station between despair and hope, where the elders could gradually recuperate from their trauma and prepare to return to a normal life.

My mother, Renée, and I set out from Genova in our little white rented Fiat Uno. We had no difficulty following the map to Grugliasco, just to the southwest of Torino. However, instead of the quaint town beyond the city that my mother remembered, we found a densely built new residential suburb of Torino. Architecturally undistinguished, virtually identical apartment blocks had replaced the charming old houses, and she was unable to recognize any of the streets. We were greeted by curious stares: Grugliasco was obviously not a place that attracted many tourists. My mother tried to explain to several people, in Italian gone rusty from long years of disuse, that we were looking for the camp where the Jews had lived after the Second World War. The invariable response was a shrug of the shoulders and a quizzical expression. We knew that the last Jewish residents had left the camp by the early fifties, but we had no idea what had become of the place afterwards, or even if the buildings were still standing. My mother had a vivid recollection of the neighborhood she lived in for almost three years, but nothing looked the way she remembered it. The most helpful person we encountered was an African guest worker with a decent command of English. He directed us to the nearby *carabinieri* station, on the assumption that this would be the best place to get directions. The two young policemen on duty were mystified by our strange inquiry: What Jews? There were no Jews in Grugliasco that they knew of. After nearly an hour of driving around aimlessly, we were at our wit's end and ready to abandon the search.

Dark thoughts raced through my mind. I had grown up on my mother's stories about the camp in Grugliasco. These stories were a crucial component of my self-image as a child of survivors from Hungary who came to Canada by way of an Italian refugee camp. Is it possible that this was all just a fantasy?

I was looking for the *autostrada* that would lead us onward to Milano when we spotted an old man at the side of the road eyeing us. A final, desperate impulse struck me: Perhaps an old-timer would remember where the Jews had lived after the War? We got out of the car, and my mother posed the question to him in her fractured Italian. Ah, you mean the *ospedale psichiatrico*? Of course he knew where the psychiatric hospital was. And he certainly remembered the Jews. In fact, he remembered them quite fondly and expressed a strong identification with them. Nicola Catalano, as he introduced himself, was a swarthy Calabrese, still ill at ease and out of place among the northerners after so many years of living in their midst. He had been a Communist and a partisan who fought first against Mussolini's fascists and then against the *Wehrmacht* invaders. He knew what the Germans had done to the Jews. He regarded the Jewish survivors who straggled into Grugliasco after the War as his comrades-in-arms in the struggle against fascism, and he had been sorry to see them leave a few years later.

Without warning, Nicola burst into tears. Potent emotions, long dormant, engulfed him. When he regained his composure, he responded to our request. Yes, he would be very pleased to take us to the site of the refugee camp. We were astounded to learn from Nicola that the site was still in service as the regional psychiatric hospital. He was familiar with the hospital because his late wife had worked there as an orderly for many years. Nicola got into our car, and instructed me to turn right at the next street and proceed to the gate in the middle of the high stone wall running its length. We had been two minutes away from this inconspicuous spot, and we had driven past it several times without realizing what it was. Nicola got out and laboriously pushed open the heavy iron gate.

When we drove through, my mother gasped. Everything was exactly as she had remembered it. For my part, I was astonished to discover that the camp was not at all what I had imagined it to be. In my mind's eye, I had always pictured endless rows of austere wooden barracks on an interminable plain – a sort of benign concentration camp where the inmates did not have to worry about being gassed to death. In actuality, the psychiatric hospital of Grugliasco had architecturally distinguished stone buildings and beautifully landscaped grounds. I was informed later that in its time, it had been considered by the Italian psychiatric profession to be a state-of-the-art facility. I was also surprised to learn that the hospital was still quite new when the Jewish refugees arrived. The official inauguration had taken place in 1931, amidst considerable ceremony, in the presence of King Vittorio Emanuele III and the Governor of Piedmont.

Nicola led us to the main administrative building. At the reception desk, he announced the arrival of special guests from Canada. Within a minute, a distinguished-looking woman in a white lab coat came out to greet us. She introduced herself in English as Dr. Caterina Corbascio, a psychiatrist and the director of the hospital. Dr. Corbascio was quite taken aback by our arrival. Foreign visitors were obviously an uncommon sight at this strictly regional facility. Politely, she asked how she might help us. My mother explained that this place had been her home for almost three years after the War, before her family immigrated to Canada.

Dr. Corbascio was puzzled: Why would a mentally sound non-Italian woman have been living in a psychiatric hospital in northern Italy?

Then Dr. Corbascio noticed the blue number on my mother's forearm. She froze. She had read about Jews being tattooed by the Nazis in the concentration camps, but she had never actually met such a person. Now she knew that this stranger from Canada was telling the truth.

My mother proceeded to relate how in 1946, the United Nations Relief and Rehabilitation Administration had taken over the hospital and transformed it into a camp for Jewish refugees. She and many others had ended up here because there was simply no country in the world prepared to take them in on humanitarian grounds, even after the shocking story of the mass murder of European Jewry had become common knowledge. Dr. Corbascio was deeply shaken: devoted heart and soul to her profession and to her patients, she thought she knew all there was to know about the place where she had been working for the past fifteen years. The rather unsettling fact was that she and her colleagues had no idea whatsoever of an important chapter in the hospital's history.

A recent development led Dr. Corbascio and her co-workers to listen with particularly rapt attention to my mother's story. The election of Silvio Berlusconi as Prime Minister had stirred a heated debate throughout the country. Did this event signal a nostalgic return by Italians to the right-wing nationalism that had years earlier proved so disastrous for Italy? Dr. Corbascio had a friend, Gino Li Veli, who was a journalist at the Milanese newspaper, *La Repubblica*. She knew him to be distraught at the country's turn to the political right, toward what he saw as a narrow and mean-spirited chauvinism. She was sure Gino would jump at the opportunity to write about Jews from Canada who had been warmly received by Italians after the War, and who had come back these many years later to express their gratitude. He and a photographer met us on our arrival in Milano, and a few days later, my mother enjoyed her moment of fame in the Italian press.[2]

She welcomed this unexpected opportunity to thank the Italian people publicly for their kindness to the Jewish refugees after the War. To this day, she proudly shows people the article and relates the story behind it with great enthusiasm.

In the years since that first visit to Grugliasco, Caterina Corbascio has kept her promise to stay in touch with my mother, to whom she still sends a greeting card every Christmas.

In Search of the *Piccolo Polacchino*

Eight years after rediscovering Grugliasco, we were surprised to receive a package from Italy containing a letter and a book. Dr. Massimo Moraglio, a historian at the University of Torino, had just published a scholarly study titled *Costruire il manicomio: Storia dell'ospedale psichiatrico di Grugliasco* (Building the Asylum: A History of the Psychiatric Hospital of Grugliasco). In the course of researching his subject, he had occasion to interview the director of the hospital, Dr. Caterina Corbascio. From her, he had learned of our visit and of the dramatic disclosure that the hospital complex had once housed a camp for Jewish refugees. Dr. Moraglio thought we might appreciate having a copy of his book.

I thanked Dr. Moraglio by e-mail for his gracious gift, and he replied as follows:

> I can confirm that the subject of the treatment of Jewish refugees in Italy after the Second World War has been neglected and not studied at all. Almost no one, including the historians, remembers the fact that Italy, a country that under fascism had been allied with Nazi Germany, had given temporary hospitality to refugees who survived the concentration camps. The memory has been lost. During my research regarding the hospital of Grugliasco, it was very difficult to trace the passage of the refugees, which I briefly reported in my book... I hope to be able in the coming years to contribute in researching this subject, and your help will be precious.[1]

Here was an academic work of two hundred pages, presenting the history of the hospital in exacting detail – but barely mentioning the single most interesting fact about it. The following is the sum total of what Dr. Moraglio wrote about the Jewish refugees in Grugliasco:

> In August 1945, with the establishment of the UNRRA, the hospital was used as a camp for the assembly and relocation of Jewish refugees from Eastern Europe. Thousands came to the center in Grugliasco in the hope of being able to leave for destinations overseas. This lasted until October 1949, after the ILO had been established. First, the Germans, then the Allies, and finally the last Jewish residents abandoned the complex.[2]

Dr. Moraglio was intrigued to learn about the mysterious lapse of memory among his compatriots, and he was determined to have the story of the Grugliasco refugees researched properly.

A year later, Dr. Moraglio was very pleased to announce that he had identified the right person to fill the gap in his work. Sara Vinçon was a graduate student in the department of history at the University of Torino. Under the guidance of her supervisor, Professor Fabio Levi, she was writing a dissertation on the subject of the displaced persons' camp in Grugliasco. "Would you and your mother be prepared to provide Ms. Vinçon with any information in your possession concerning the camp?" Dr. Moraglio wished to know. "Of course," I responded, "We would be more than happy to do so."

Upon establishing an e-mail correspondence with Sara, I learned that she had developed a special interest in the postwar Jewish refugees because of her own unusual story. She had been born into a family of Waldensians, Protestants of French origin living in the Piedmont region of Italy. Since the age of twelve, she had felt deeply, for reasons she herself could not fathom, that it was her destiny to be a Jew. It came as no surprise that Sara's eventual conversion to Judaism seriously complicated her life. As a Protestant in overwhelmingly Roman Catholic Italy, she had always been regarded as a heretic. Now, as a Jew, she was regarded as something even worse – an apostate. She was also the only child of her parents, who lived in the village of San Germano Chisone. Growing up, she had never encountered an actual Jewish person, but Sara was probably influenced by the affinity that Waldensians felt with Jews, the other religious minority of any consequence in Italy. Waldensians were very conscious of the fact that they shared with Jews a long parallel history of persecution at the hands of the Roman Catholic Church. They were also granted full rights of citizenship at the same time as the Jews, in 1848, under King Carlo Alberto of Piedmont. During the German occupation of Italy toward the end of the Second World War, many Waldensians hid Jewish fugitives in the same mountain valleys where their own ancestors had found refuge in earlier generations.

When she enrolled as a student at the University of Torino, Sara finally had the opportunity to meet flesh-and-blood Jews. She embraced the members of the small Jewish community of Torino as her new kin, and they were glad to reciprocate her affection. These people she now drew into her life were proud of the long and glorious history of their ancestors in Italy, and specifically in the Piedmont region. However, in the characteristic Italian fashion, their well-defined ethnic consciousness went hand-in-hand with a pronounced laxity in religious observance. Before long, having been attracted to Judaism as a religion rather than as an ethnic identity, Sara found herself in the curious position of being one of the very few religiously observant members of the Torino community.

Sara was fascinated to learn from some of the older people in the community that thousands of Jewish refugees had temporarily lived in the region after the War. At any given moment, there were about three thousand Jews to be found in the Grugliasco displaced persons' camp. By coincidence, this was the same number as the membership of the established Jewish community of Torino at the time. Much like her, the foreign Jews in the camp were strangers driven by some inscrutable destiny to this particular place. Piecing together the refugees' untold story and vicariously reliving their experiences satisfied a profound personal need within her.

Sara proceeded to research her subject with great energy and enthusiasm. She found many interesting documents in the state, municipal, and Jewish community archives. As she progressed with her work, she was amazed at the sheer volume of these materials. A number of Sara's discoveries eventually proved helpful to me in my own quest to comprehend my origins.

This is not to suggest that Sara had an easy time gaining access to the documents in question. To her surprise, she found the Benvenuto and Alessandro Terracini Archive of the Jewish community of Torino the most difficult to penetrate. For some reason, the community leaders considered certain documents "sensitive." These were not catalogued, and were securely stored away in one of the two massive towers flanking the synagogue and looming over the neighborhood. Being a very determined individual, Sara somehow persuaded someone to let her see part of what was hidden away in the towers. By her own account, she was humorously described within the tightly-knit Jewish community as being like Raponserola (Rapunzel) climbing down from the tower on her long braid. I was intrigued: What dark secret could these people be harboring?

It struck me that while I considered myself a proud son of Torino, in actuality, I was an outsider. I decided to learn more about the people in whose midst I had been born. Sara, the courageous young Jew-by-choice who had started out as far more of an outsider than I, was to serve as my guide to the Torino Jewish community.

Besides their infant son, everything my parents possessed when they arrived in Toronto was contained in two knapsacks. My mother had not been able to salvage a single memento from her former life, as the sullen squatters who had commandeered her family's home in Szerencs refused to allow her past the front door. My father was free to remove whatever he wished from his home in Szentistvan, but because of the clandestine departure and the blind journey ahead, the members of the group decided to take only what they could readily carry on their backs. The two knapsacks belonging to my parents contained a set of bed-linens, a hand-embroidered table-cloth, some pots and pans, several Rubinstein family photographs, and a small rug my father had woven to calm his nerves while waiting in vain for his family's return. The only items added along the way were the *kesubah*, the traditional Jewish marriage contract hand-written in Grugliasco on a cheap piece of lined paper, and the embarkation cards for the *S.S. Sobieski*, which transported them from Genova to Halifax.

With so few artifacts from the past available to me, and with only my mother's remarkable but all-too-human memories to guide me in reconstructing the Grugliasco chronicle, I cherished every bit of new information that came my way. The richness of these new details made a once monochromatic story burst into color. They corrected, supplemented, amplified, and occasionally added poignancy to the existing story. They also provided empirical confirmation that my mother's otherwise uncorroborated testimony was not an eccentric fantasy.

Sara informed me in her very first e-mail that she had already conducted research on all of the male babies born to Jewish parents in the Grugliasco camp. She had done this by examining the circumcision register of the Torino Jewish community as well as the corresponding birth certificates at the Grugliasco town hall. She e-mailed the entries pertaining to me, in the Italian originals accompanied by her English translation.[3]

From the circumcision register:

#964 – Rubinstein Elia Mordechai, whose parents are Dov and Schwartz Judith, was born in the Maria Vittoria Hospital in Torino on March 5, 1948, at 17.00 and circumcised there on March 12, 1948, (a Saturday) by Prof. Dr. Giulio Segre in the presence of Rabbi Della Pergola.[4]

And from the birth certificate:

Rubinstein Robert, born on 5 March 1948 at 19:00 at the Maria Vittoria Hospital, of Schwarcz Judith, 27 years old, a seamstress by profession, a Hungarian citizen, resident in Grugliasco, married to Rubinstein Béla, 38 years old, a miller by profession, a Hungarian citizen, and resident in Grugliasco.[5]

I had grown up on my mother's assertion that a local Jewish physician by the name of Professor Doctor Levi had performed my circumcision. I was glad to possess this one specific detail regarding my earliest days, in the absence of so many others. Now I was startled to learn that the physician's name was actually Professor Doctor Giulio Segre. Sara thought that my mother probably confused him with Signor Isacco Levi, a beloved lay activist in the Torino Jewish community. It would appear that this gentleman was involved in arranging circumcisions for the Jewish boys born at the Maria Vittoria Hospital. I imagined that part of his procedure was to pay a congratulatory visit to each new mother. As my mother's Italian was rather limited and Signor Levi's Hungarian was surely non-existent, there would have been room for confusion in their conversation. Since childbearing women were regarded in those days as invalids needing two weeks of bed-rest, my mother would not have been present at the actual circumcision, which was performed elsewhere in the hospital. It was perfectly plausible that she should have thought her congenial visitor to be the *mohel*.

Sara also reported that according to Chief Rabbi Luciano Caro of Ferrara, who was a teenager at the time and remembers the good doctor well, I should recite the *birkat ha-gomel*, the traditional prayer for redemption from danger, because by the time of my circumcision, Professor Doctor Segre was a very elderly gentleman with a severe tremor in his hand.[6]

My mother may have been confused about the name of the doctor who performed my circumcision, but she had no recollection whatsoever regarding the name of the rabbi who officiated at her wedding in Grugliasco. She did remember that the rabbi was a native of Yugoslavia and a fellow resident of Grugliasco. A fervent religious Zionist, he was patiently waiting his turn to leave for *Eretz Yisrael* in the middle of the night.

Thanks to Anna, the secretary of Chief Rabbi Somekh, Sara was able to obtain a copy of the wedding record for the refugee camps in the region. The document contained a declaration by Rabbi Disegni, the Chief Rabbi of Torino at the time, in which he recognized the validity of the weddings performed in Grugliasco and nearby Rivoli. He also authorized Rabbi Laurenzio Hartman to continue officiating at these weddings. Rabbi Disegni requested that the names of the couples married in the camps be transmitted to the Jewish Community of Torino for inclusion in the master registry of all Jewish marriages. This indicated that the weddings in the camps were considered equal in validity to those of the old Torinese, and the refugees were being included in the community, at least for ritual purposes.[7]

My mother was pleased to have yet another gap in her memory filled, and to recognize the name of the rabbi who officiated at her wedding in Grugliasco as Laurenzio Hartman.

The story about refugees who rode the trains in Italy using homemade tickets bearing a "Kosher" certification stamp is one of my favorites. My mother always offered, as an appendix to the story, an explanation as to why the conductors honored these obviously counterfeit tickets. The way she saw it, the Italian people were very kind to the Jewish strangers in their midst, and this story is a characteristic illustration of their decency. I was therefore surprised to learn from Sara that she had discovered in the Benvenuto and Alessandro Terracini Archive a rather difficult exchange of letters between officials of the Italian Railway and representatives of the Torino Jewish community. It seems that a conductor had caught several refugees riding without tickets. When he demanded the home addresses of the travelers, in order to mail notices of fines to them, they declared that they were members of the Jewish community of Torino, and that this community was responsible for them. Consequently, the Italian Railway officials wrote to the Torino Jewish community demanding payment for the train rides. The communal representatives wrote back expressing regret at the unflattering image of Jews caused by this incident. They pointed out that the miscreants were actually foreign Jews living temporarily in the Grugliasco refugee camp, and they denied all responsibility for the actions of the transient neighbors with whom they merely happened to share an ancestral religion.

In addition to correcting errors in my mother's reconstruction of the past, Sara has been able to coax out long submerged memories, sometimes with amusing effect. For example, she once asked me to find out whether my mother remembered anything about people in the refugee camp chopping wood in their sleeping quarters. This struck me as a rather odd question, but when I posed it to my mother, her eyes lit up. "Yes, of course, it is true!" She explained by relating the following story:

The central kitchen in Grugliasco was used to prepare communal meals for everyone in the camp. In the early days, an exception was made for the small minority of residents who observed the Jewish dietary laws. A tiny kosher kitchen was set up, and a *shoichet*, a Jewish ritual slaughterer, was assigned to the camp to provide a regular supply of fresh kosher meat. The meat served to everyone else was military-issue canned beef from America, heavily salted and floating in fat. Word quickly spread through the camp that the kosher meat was of much better quality, and the demand for it exploded. The authorities were unable to satisfy the demand, and they were anxious to avoid charges of treating residents unequally. They were probably also put off by the hypocrisy of the many suddenly pious residents. It was decided to discontinue the provision of kosher meat and to close down the kosher kitchen.

The number of residents observing the Jewish dietary laws dropped back to the previous low level. The diehards were left with no choice but to buy their own live chickens in town and slaughter them with a straightedge razor. The camp administrators failed to realize, or perhaps no longer cared, that those who conscientiously kept kosher were compelled to find a separate place to prepare their food. One enterprising individual came up with a clever if unauthorized solution: He removed a large metal garbage drum from the grounds, dragged it into his dormitory room, and placed it upside-down next to the window. He cut an opening at the bottom for inserting firewood, and a smaller one on top connected to a hose venting smoke out the window. The kosher chickens were cooked on the top surface of the inverted drum. The "firewood" came from unused bunk beds stored in one of the dormitories. It was chopped up on the floor right there in the room.

When Captain Davidge, the British officer in charge of administering the camp, found out about the improvised kosher kitchen, he wrote in his report: "People who are this resourceful should have no difficulty finding their way in the world."

How did Sara know about the woodcutting story? In the course of her research, she had come across certain records stored in the Province of Torino Archive. The regional authorities had been quite upset about the commandeering of their psychiatric hospital, first by the German army, then by the British occupation forces, then by the International Red Cross, and finally by the United Nations Relief and Rehabilitation Administration. They had to scramble to relocate the patients to alternative quarters, and, adding insult to injury, no one ever offered to pay the rightful owners rent for the use of the facilities. The ultimate indignity was to learn that some of the refugees encamped in the hospital were chopping up furniture for firewood and burning it indoors in a garbage drum. In an insistent memorandum to the British administrators, the regional authorities demanded to know who was going to take responsibility for the destruction of their property. They also demanded to know when they might expect to get their hospital back. In all fairness, the officials did indicate several times, in quintessentially civilized Italian fashion, that they were aware of what the Germans had done to the Jews and that they commiserated with these wretched people. By no account does this mean, however, that the Italian bureaucrats accepted responsibility for sheltering the refugees, or offered to find them alternative living quarters.

Thanks to Sara, I have learned many interesting facts about the camp in Grugliasco. Virtually everything that I knew previously was based upon what my mother had told me, as no one else in the family ever talked about the years in Italy. Of course, her perspective as a marginalized, linguistically challenged outsider limited her knowledge of what was happening around her. She also obviously lacked access to official communications. Sara's examination of archival materials has added a whole new dimension to my mother's vivid recollections, subjective as they are, and prone as they have been to shifting with the passage of time.

The Grugliasco I was getting to know quite well was a rather different place than the Grugliasco I had discovered a decade earlier in 1994. On the first trip, my mother, Renée, and I had stumbled about like three blind mice. We had no idea what became of the refugee camp after September 1948 when the family left for Canada. The town itself had been transformed beyond recognition by post-war urban sprawl. Thanks only to a chance encounter at our moment of despair did we discover what remained of the camp. We also learned, to our wonder, that the inhabitants of Grugliasco had lost all remembrance of the Jewish refugees who once lived in their midst.

As an indirect consequence of the initial contact with Dr. Caterina Corbascio, I discovered that there was a functioning Jewish community in Torino. With Sara Vinçon's help, I started to connect with its members. I resolved to return to my birthplace once more, to reconsider it from a fresh perspective deepened by newly acquired information.

As much as my mother would have loved to join us for the reunion, this time she was simply not up to it. She was now eighty-four years old, and the intervening decade had not been kind to her health. Besides, she was reluctant to leave my father, who was ninety-six years old, housebound, and increasingly dependent on her. Renée and I decided to take our younger son Erez with us, thereby introducing a member of the third generation to Grugliasco for the first time.

We learned from Caterina that the psychiatric hospital had been closed down six and a half years earlier and the patients transferred to more up-to-date facilities in the region. She was now in private practice and her office, by pure coincidence, was located in the old Jewish district near the synagogue. I asked Caterina if she thought it might be possible for us to visit the hospital site. She responded that she was not sure the police would allow us to enter.

I was fascinated to learn the reason: Illegal immigrants from Albania and Romania had taken shelter in one of the buildings. The immigration authorities knew exactly where they were, and voiced disapproval at the manner in which they had chosen to arrive in Italy. In practice, however, the authorities looked the other way, pending official resolution of the newcomers' status. Unlike an earlier generation of strangers who had lived in the very same place, these people had not been persecuted back home: they were simply economic migrants who had come to Italy in the hope of finding work and raising their standard of living.

Upon further inquiry, Caterina was pleased to report that there would be no problem entering the site. The police considered the illegal immigrants to be perfectly harmless.

The morning after our arrival in Torino, Caterina picked us up at the hotel and drove us to Grugliasco. I could not help but note the sheer effortlessness of getting there this time. I also kept thinking back to the tortuous wanderings that had led my family to this sanctuary so many years before.

What was it about the place? Caterina speculated that although the buildings had been designed as a haven for mentally ill Italians, it seemed their true destiny was to serve as a transit point for foreigners dreaming of a better life. She asked me what I thought of her theory. I shrugged. *Who knows?* Certainly, everything about my own family's remarkable experience suggested that she was on the right track.

We drove through the open gate. There before us was the campus of the psychiatric hospital of Grugliasco, just as it had been when we saw it a decade earlier, just as it had been when I entered the world in 1948, and just as it had been when King Vittorio Emanuele III arrived for the festive dedication in 1931. Human beings are ephemeral, but the structures they erect can endure for a very long time.

Yet, a closer look revealed that the place was not the same as it had once been. The formerly handsome buildings were now a sorry sight, their windows smashed, and the interiors ransacked. Garbage and debris were strewn about the grounds. I stared at the peeling, crumbling entrance to the 'D' dormitory building that had been my very first home. I visualized a pale blond infant lying on the lawn at the front of the building, basking in the summer sun with his doting parents.

I turned and gazed out at the large field adjoining the main gate leading into the compound. The oak trees ringing the field were still there, tall and proud, but weeds had overwhelmed the lawn. The high brick wall along the outside edge of the field was still intact, with an ageless massiveness suggesting that it would go on sheltering all within, as it had always done. It mattered not whether those inside were psychiatric patients or refugees, whether they were Italian, Jewish, Romanian, or Albanian. The one anachronistic feature in the scene was the cluster of newly constructed high-rise apartment buildings looming outside the wall in the everyday world beyond.

I focused all my psychic energy on the sights before me, filtering out the obtrusive new structures and summoning up a vision of a crowd filling the field. The people were gathering around a *hupah*, a traditional Jewish marriage canopy. Under the *hupah* stood the bride and groom. Just as in the faded old photograph, the bride looked radiant while the groom looked melancholy.

I felt hidden eyes staring at me, curious yet fearful. I sensed the Albanians and Romanians watching me from their windows, wondering to themselves: "Who is this tall, distracted-looking stranger, and why would he be so interested in this pathetic place? Perhaps the authorities sent him to find us?" The poor souls could not possibly understand me, not at this stage of their odyssey. For my part, as the son of my parents, I felt that I understood their anxieties very well indeed. I silently wished them good luck in their quest to build better lives for themselves and their families.

The Jewish communities of Torino and Szerencs were as different from one another as day and night. The first exemplified the successful integration of long-time inhabitants into the mainstream of Italian society. The second exemplified the insecurities of recent immigrants in search of economic betterment and freedom from persecution, who were eager to believe that they could be as Hungarian as anyone else. Yet, when both cities fell under direct German domination toward the end of the War, their destinies were suddenly linked in a bizarre Tale of Two Cities. Just as the tide began to turn against Germany and hopes were raised that those European Jews still living would be spared the fate of millions of their brethren, the deportations from both Torino and Szerencs commenced with a vengeance.

The Jews of Torino arrived at Auschwitz in February 1944, four months before Judit Schwarcz and her family and the rest of the Jews of Szerencs. Whatever the differences between the Italians and the Hungarians before they arrived on the notorious train platform, they were indistinguishable once clad in gray-and-white-striped prisoners' pajamas.

No human being could ever be properly prepared for the concentration camp experience, but the Jews of Torino were in a state of shocked paralysis. Because of their thorough integration into Italian life, most of them had been hopelessly naïve about the Germans' malevolent intentions towards them.

The Torinese Jews had once formed an extraordinarily affluent community. By 1624, there were nine Jewish merchant banks in Torino, and Jews became leading traders in silks and wool. By the 1860's, the migration from smaller towns had brought the city's Jewish population to nearly four thousand five hundred, and their degree of wealth and influence was unmatched in Europe.

The defining symbol of Torino is a towering structure known as the *Mole Antonelliana,* "Antonelli's pile." Today, it houses the National Museum of Cinema, but when construction commenced in 1863, it was intended to be a synagogue. The Jewish community of the day was so infatuated with its newfound status that it decided to build a House of God of unparalleled grandeur. The architect, Alessandro Antonelli, was swept up in the enthusiasm, and kept expanding his building until it was grotesquely disproportional to its surroundings. In the end, even the affluent Jews of Torino had their financial limits. Facing horrendous cost overruns, and realizing that their grandiose project was drawing animosity rather than admiration from the Catholic majority, they sold the building to the municipality. In 1884, a chastened Jewish community built the far more sensibly scaled "*Tempio Israelitico,*" the Jewish temple.

When Mussolini came to power in 1922, plenty of Jews ardently supported the fascist enterprise. However, most Jews were anti-fascists and some became resistance fighters. When the Germans seized control of Italy after the collapse of Mussolini's government, they were not interested in the politics of the Torinese Jews. Jewish fascists and anti-fascists alike were shipped to Auschwitz, and hardly any returned.

On Shabbat, Renée, Erez, and I attended services at the Tempio Israelitico, and experienced the beautiful liturgical traditions unique to Torino. Not only do the Italian Jews have their own distinctive liturgy, but also

each separate community has its own specific variations. Our hosts pointed out, on a wall of the soaring sanctuary, a large brass plaque dedicated to
the memory of Isacco Levi. I certainly recognized the name of the gentleman who, in my mind, had arranged circumcisions for the baby boys in
the Grugliasco camp, including me. We were told that the Jews of Torino
remember Signor Levi with deep gratitude for his contribution to the rebuilding of their community after the War. They especially remember the
sweet way he introduced the young people to the riches of the Jewish tradition through the *Bar* and *Bat Mitzvah* lessons he taught for so many years.

We were invited to a traditional Friday evening dinner at the home
of Franco and Alda Segre, leaders of the community, who had assembled
a distinguished group of Torinese Jews to join us. Among them was Tullio
Levi, a member of the Jewish Studies Group that publishes *Ha-Keillah*,
the journal of the Torino Jewish community. He asked me if I would be
willing to be interviewed for the upcoming issue regarding my family's
experience in the Grugliasco camp. I agreed gladly.[8]

Another guest was Signora Giulia Colombo Diena, the cousin and
childhood companion of Primo Levi. With Sara translating, this elegant
and distinguished lady told us how the Jews of Torino had been so thoroughly assimilated that, had the fascist era and the War not come along,
they would by now have disappeared completely as Jews. The events of
the day forced the members of the community to re-examine and reaf-
firm their Jewish identity.

Signora Diena related that when the Jewish refugees began arriving
in Torino after the War, the community organized a committee to assist
them, and she served as a volunteer. She and her friends gave freely of
their time and energy to help the refugees in whatever ways they could.
The American Jewish Joint Distribution Committee regularly provided
the leaders of the community with funds, to be disbursed to the needy
refugees at their discretion.

We learned from Signora Diena that members of the Jewish Brigade, who were investing most of their efforts in Zionist education and
the smuggling of Jewish refugees into Palestine, had also made regular
deliveries of clothing and food to the community offices. As both the lay
leadership and the Rabbinate of the Torino community were staunchly
anti-Zionist, they refused to have any official contact with the Brigade.
Yet, in light of the pressing humanitarian challenge, they could not turn

down the offers of assistance. Signora Diena giggled mischievously as she described the time she took delivery at the community offices of a huge quantity of lard acquired somehow by the Brigade. She and her friends had to hide it away from the eyes of Rabbi Disegni until it could be traded for food. She never did discover where those nice Jewish boys found all that pig-fat with which to help their fellow Jews.

Sara told me afterwards that only a relatively small number of people came to the Torino community looking for help, almost always of the monetary sort. These people tended to be aggressive, and often quite shameless. Some of them received money and then came back later using false names, trying to collect additional funds. When they were caught in the act, they sniveled melodramatically about their suffering during the War. They did not seem to realize, or care, that the Jews of Torino had endured their own hell at the hands of the Germans.

When I mentioned the Torino assistance committee to my mother upon our return to Toronto, she expressed disdain. She and the other members of the family would have been mortified to ask for money. Unhappy as they were to be trapped in the camp, their basic needs were being met. They had food, shelter, and clothing without making the slightest effort, but they were humiliated anew each day to have to accept these unearned gifts. All they wanted was the opportunity to work, so that they might provide for themselves with dignity.

As we spoke, it struck me that Signora Diena was the first member of the Torino Jewish community who was able to give me an eyewitness account of the Grugliasco camp. I asked her whether she knew Signora Finzi, who had unwittingly prepared the men of my family for their jobs as furriers in Canada by teaching them how to cut pieces of leather. Yes, she did indeed remember the lady. The two women had been quite friendly, but after the War, the purse-maker had closed her shop and gone to live with relatives in Rome. Signora Diena had not heard any news of Signora Finzi in many years, and given her advanced age, she had in all likelihood died. I would have loved to meet someone in the Torino Jewish community who actually knew my parents. Alas, Signora Finzi's name was the only one my mother could recall.

The members of the Torino Jewish community were warm and friendly, and eager to engage in conversation. They had many questions about our life in Toronto, but above all, they were curious to know what my family did for a living. When I informed them that we were real estate developers, these Jews of Torino could not hide their astonishment. They clearly had difficulty reconciling the new image of prosperous business-men with memories of the pitiful refugees of so long ago.

I felt an urge to bond with these people who were born in the same place as me. At the same time, it struck me how utterly different the Tori-nese Jews were from my own family. I speculated about alternate realities: had Italy's economy not been devastated after the War, had the govern-ment invited the Jewish refugees to stay, I might well have grown up and made my life among these people. *Would we eventually have assimilated and turned into Torinese Jews, or would we instead have had a transforma-tive effect on the community, as was to be the case in Toronto?*

Life can be full of surprises. After all the wandering and uncertainty, my parents would have jumped at the opportunity to settle into a normal existence in Torino. Yet, distressing as their rootlessness must have been at the time, it ultimately proved a blessing that they could not stay in Italy. That they ended up instead in far-off Canada proved to be the best thing that could have happened to them.

After returning from Italy, we maintained regular contact with Sara, continuing to share information and keeping up with family events. She gladly accepted our invitation to spend the upcoming Passover holiday with us in Toronto. On this quintessentially familial Jewish festival, she truly became a member of our family. After many months of disembod-ied telephone conversation, Sara and my mother finally met in person, and predictably, they hit it off beautifully. The long, heartfelt dialogues that ensued filled a deep need in both of them.

In October 2005, Sara's dissertation, "Lives in Transit: The Story of the Refugee Camp of Grugliasco (1945–1949)"[9] was accepted by the De-partment of History at the University of Torino. The Rubinstein family of Toronto, Canada shared in her pride at this achievement.

How It Really Was

When I learned from Sara at the beginning of our correspondence that my *mohel's* name was not "Levi" but "Segre," I assumed that if my mother remembered the name "Levi," it must have been because someone by this name had visited her at the hospital. With her weak Italian, she could easily have been confused about the identity of her visitor. Since Isacco Levi was a well-known lay activist in the Torino Jewish community, as Sara had informed me, I conjectured that he must have been the person who arranged circumcisions for the baby boys of Grugliasco. I envisaged a jolly, rotund gentleman speaking animated Italian showing up every day at the Maria Vittoria maternity ward. He would seek out any Jewish refugee woman who had just given birth to a son, planting an exuberant Italian kiss on both her cheeks and promising to arrange the circumcision ceremony. He would wish her a heartfelt *mazal tov* in the name of her fellow Jews in the Torino community who shared her joy at this special time.

Something about this narrative did not feel right. When we returned to Toronto from Italy, I asked my mother whether she remembered anyone from the Torino Jewish community visiting her in the Maria Vittoria maternity ward. She responded without hesitation that no one other than members of the family had come to see her at the hospital. In fact, aside from Signora Finzi, she could not recall *ever* meeting a member of the Torino Jewish community. Just to be certain, I repeated the question and asked her to think about it very carefully. My mother proclaimed unequivocally: no Torinese ever came to visit her at the hospital.

Alas, the Isacco-Levy-in-the-maternity-ward scenario was a figment of my eager imagination. Thinking back, I ask myself: why had I been so quick to conjure it up?

I grew up influenced by my mother's praise for the civility and warmth of the Italians among whom she had once lived. For me, Italy was the key to all the blessings that subsequently befell my family. It was there that my parents regained their faith in humanity and mustered the resolve to rebuild their shattered lives. For a very long time, I had an unrealistic tendency to assume the best about any Italian whom I encountered.

Now older and wiser, I have learned that the reality is far more nuanced than my wishful fantasy. It seems that just as victims of persecution and degradation in search of healing sometimes impose helpful mythologies upon the objective facts, so do their children who yearn to understand them.

The Jews of Torino were really no better or worse than the Jews of Toronto in their treatment of the refugees in their midst (no better or worse, for that matter, than people anywhere who find strangers suddenly appearing on their doorstep). As a rule, long-time residents act haughtily toward immigrants, regarding them as socially and economically inferior. There is always something disquieting about strangers speaking alien tongues, wearing peculiar clothing and perhaps smelling oddly.

Did Isacco Levi actually meet my mother? We shall probably never know. People in Torino who knew him personally confirm that Isacco Levi was a very special man, dedicated to his beloved Torino Jewish community. I had managed to convince myself that he must also have felt an affinity with other Jews, and particularly those who had survived the Nazi onslaught in common with his own compatriots. As a traditional Jew, he would have considered it a *mitzvah,* a religious imperative, to assist the refugees living in nearby Grugliasco. But, it is clear to me now, even if he did arrange circumcision ceremonies for the refugees, this does not mean that he or any of his fellow Torinese felt obliged to engage these people socially at even the most elementary level.

I kept thinking back to what Sara had told me about the secretiveness of the Torino Jewish community. She had encountered serious resistance when she sought access to the archives stored in the synagogue tower. *What were the Jews of Torino hiding?* Most likely, I have concluded, they were covering up the dishonorable behavior of certain members of the community during the fascist regime.

This would tie in with the broader mystery of the collective amnesia of the Italian people, or at least of those living in the Torino region. I first became aware of the phenomenon when we were searching in vain for the site of the camp on our first visit to Grugliasco. It was further illustrated by the total ignorance of the hospital staff regarding the facility's one-time Jewish occupants, and it received scholarly confirmation from the local historian, Dr. Massimo Moraglio.

Why did the Italians forget about the refugees living in their midst? How was it even possible to lose all trace of such a notable story, and so soon after the fact? The sheltering of Jewish survivors after the War surely reflects favorably on the people of Italy, even if it was not their initiative. One would expect them to recall this period with at least mild pride, not to banish it from their memories as if it were shameful.

The answer may lie in the Italians' perception of the refugee camps. They may well have regarded the camps as a humiliating punishment imposed upon them by the Allies for their association with Nazi Germany. They understood that on account of this ignominious liaison, the victors considered the Italian people indirectly responsible for the horrific consequences of the Germans' murderous campaign against the Jews.

I now know that the Italians are hardly the nation of saints that my mother has always depicted. Like the Germans, they are, on the whole and under normal circumstances, a refined people proud of their image as standard-bearers of civilization. Nevertheless, in the morally perverted environment of fascist Italy, large numbers of them proved capable of betraying the norms of civilized behavior.

In fairness, the fascist government of Italy never quite sank to the depraved level of Nazi Germany. Mussolini is reported to have told Hitler that just as he had no business telling the Fuehrer what to do with the Jews under German rule, the Fuehrer should not presume to tell *him* what to do with *his* Jews. It is a shameful fact that the fascists did arrest Jews and intern them in prisons and concentration camps. However, it was only after the collapse of the Italian government in September 1943, when Germany seized control of the country to prevent it from going over to the Allies, that the Germans were able to deport the Jews of Italy to the death camps.

The treatment of the Jews under the fascists is an undeniable stain on the honor of the Italian people, and an affront to their self-image. When the fascists first rose to power, the Jews of Italy, always ardent patriots, were welcomed into the movement. Many responded warmly to the call, notably Ettore Ovazza, a member of the most prominent and powerful Jewish family in Torino. However, as time went on, Mussolini proved to be an unprincipled opportunist who turned against the Jews when it suited his interests. His government passed the first of a series of anti-Semitic laws in September 1938, and they were fully in place by November. These laws subjected the forty-eight thousand Jews of Italy to a wide range of restrictions. Among other things, they barred Jewish students and teachers from public schools and universities. They prohibited Jews from marrying non-Jews, working in a long list of professions, serving in the army, employing Christian servants, staying in hotels or vacationing at resorts, and even prevented them from placing classified ads in newspapers. Thousands of Jews fled the country, no longer feeling welcome or safe in the land that had been their haven for two millennia.

There is no avoiding the unpleasant fact that in 1938, hardly anyone raised a voice in protest against the racist laws targeting Jews, much less tried to combat these laws actively. By the time the Nazis finally came for the Jews, the work of identification and concentration had already been completed. The lists of "non-Aryan" people compiled by the Mussolini government became available to the *Gestapo*, greatly facilitating the task of rounding them up. The tragic result was that eight thousand Jews were deported to their deaths.

This was certainly enough to give upright Italians a guilty conscience and a desire that the source of their discomfort disappear. For a great many of them, the most effective way to cope with the unpleasant memories was simply to banish them from consciousness.

One day, I received a package in the mail. Sara had sent me a copy of a *Siddur* "following the Italian rite specific to the holy Jewish community of Torino" so that, as she put it, from now on I could pray in harmony with my Torinese brethren. The original edition of this prayer book, with the traditional Hebrew text and a new Italian translation on facing pages, had been published in 1949, shortly after I was born and at the time that the community was struggling to re-establish itself. The present edition was a reprint from 1995.

I was struck by the double dedication opposite the title page. The Ovazza family took the lead in contributing funds toward the publication in memory of Advocate Alfredo Ovazza, who had been a prominent leader of the Jewish community. I could not help recalling that this gentleman was also the brother of the far more prominent Ettore Ovazza, the fervent champion of fascism.

In addition, Mr. Isacco Levi supported the prayer book project in memory of his tragically deceased son Daniele. I was stunned to read this. There was no indication as to when Daniele died, and under what circumstances. My imagination took flight: *Is it possible that the father undertook a circumcision campaign among the refugees as a memorial to his son?* My mother's magnanimity of spirit seizes me. Whatever the objective truth concerning Isacco Levi, I shall always be grateful to him for ushering me, along with the other five hundred and fifty baby boys of Grugliasco, into the Covenant of our Father Abraham.

During our stay in Torino, Renée, Erez, and I were invited to visit the home of a distinguished professor who was a good friend of one of our contacts. He was a very bright and learned individual, and like most members of the Italian intelligentsia, he leaned sharply to the left in his political views. He radiated empathy towards us, and evinced great interest in the Grugliasco displaced persons camp and my family's experiences there. He was particularly interested to know what my parents and the other Jewish refugees thought of the Italians they had encountered during their sojourn in his country. I was pleased to tell the professor (and he was certainly pleased to hear) that my parents held the Italian people in high esteem, and credited them with facilitating their rehabilitation after the War. I rationalized to myself that this was an accurate representation of my parents' view of things, even if I no longer shared it. The guest simply wished to reciprocate the graciousness of his host.

In the course of conversation, I mentioned that our daughter Tamar lived in Israel with her family, and that she was a student at the Tel-Aviv University School of Medicine. The professor raised his eyebrows, politely refraining from saying what I was sure he was thinking on the subject of Israel. I felt a compulsion to challenge him, although he had not actually said anything. I remarked that I was in awe of the way this valiant little country, beset by so many problems, still managed to be a world leader in many fields, including medicine, and contained some of the best universities in the world. The professor hesitated for a moment and rolled his eyes before responding. "Yes indeed. I have a colleague in the United States who emigrated from Russia via Israel. He tells me the universities in Israel are absolutely brutal, totally inhuman in the demands they make of students."

It took me a moment to realize that this was meant not as a compliment, but as a stinging reproach. I was stunned: *How do you respond to a scholar who faults others for setting rigorous academic standards? Would he dream, I wonder, of criticizing any other nation besides Israel for the pursuit of scholastic excellence?* I was deeply troubled by this encounter. On one hand, the professor displayed all the stereotypical positive traits of the Italian people on which my mother had raised me. He radiated compassion for the trace of downtrodden refugee he detected in me. On the other hand, he had difficulty accepting the significant part of me that was a prosperous member of the bourgeoisie with well-educated children.

In June 2005, the B'nai B'rith Anti-Defamation League released its annual poll examining European attitudes towards Jews. The results, sixty years after the Second World War, are deeply disturbing. Given my upbringing, there was a time when I would have expected Italy to stand out in the list as an exemplar of philo-Semitism. Today, I am saddened, but not really surprised, to find that Italy fits right in with the rest of Europe.

According to the poll, a majority of Italians believe Jews are more loyal to Israel than to their own country. An alarmingly high number of those surveyed still believe in the traditional canard that Jews have too much power in business and in international financial markets. A plurality of the Italian public continues to feel that Jews talk too much about the Holocaust, and a significant minority continues to blame Jews for the death of Jesus. In Italy, there was actually an overall increase in negative attitudes toward Jews from the 2004 findings.

The Italians, it turns out, are no different than anyone else. I keep coming back to the question: *How could my mother so distort reality by idealizing this one segment of humankind?*

I have concluded that from the standpoint of her personal experience, my mother was speaking the truth, or at least, *her* truth. She had no knowledge of the abysmal conduct described earlier, and the few individual Italians she encountered, at least the ones her subconscious mind allows her to remember, were no doubt kind-hearted and supportive.

Perhaps the Jewish refugees and the citizens of Grugliasco enjoyed a symbiotic relationship, satisfying each other's needs. The Jews enabled the Italians to redeem their sense of humanity, and the Italians enabled the Jews to regain their faith in humanity. There was probably an additional element of wish fulfillment to it: people like my parents needed desperately to believe in the essential goodness of others so that they could look optimistically to the future and start the hard work of rebuilding their lives. For this reason, they would have been inclined to give the local inhabitants the benefit of the doubt and to see only the good in them.

From the perspective of survivors struggling to regain their faith in humanity, it was not necessary for the Italians to be paragons of virtue. It was enough that they be fundamentally civilized at the moment, whatever they might have been at an earlier time, and that they relate to the Jews in their midst as they would to any other human beings, no better but also no worse.

There are various types of people in the world: some good, some bad, and the great majority indifferent to some degree. This is the commonplace view of things. But my parents and many others like them had to struggle mightily to return to this simple view from their initial despairing conclusion that mankind was evil beyond saving.

I was pondering this notion the day after Christmas, when the concierge at our hotel in Torino asked me whether I had heard about the terrible tsunami that had swept over large areas of Southeast Asia. In the days following, I was struck by the massive outpouring of sympathy and support among ordinary Italians. The fact that the victims were very far away, and vastly different from themselves in practically every respect, made no difference. The challenge of the tsunami tragedy brought out the noblest, most altruistic inclinations in Italians, as it did in people around the world.

It is not difficult to imagine that the townsfolk of Grugliasco related to the Jews in the refugee camp with the same kind of spontaneous compassion, having some sense of the horrors these people had endured just a short time before.

A few years ago, I had lunch in Tel Aviv with an Israeli businessman whom I had never met previously. Our conversation quickly revealed that we had a number of things in common. Both of his parents were survivors from Hungary, he was just a month older than I, and he had started his life in an Italian refugee camp, in Bari. I asked him when his family had come to Israel. To my great surprise, he told me that he arrived with his parents in May of 1948. I asked him how this was possible, considering that on the outbreak of the War of Independence the new government did not accept immigrants with infant children, deeming it too dangerous and lacking the resources to look after babies. He looked at me incredulously. *Who had told me such a thing?* Jews of all ages and states of health, including many small children, had arrived in a surging stream. As a matter of fundamental principle, no Jew seeking refuge would ever be turned away from the sovereign State of Israel, even in time of war.

I found this information most unsettling. I had grown up believing that the inopportune timing of my birth was the reason my parents ended up in Canada rather than Israel. Now, a chance conversation with a stranger revealed that it had not been my "fault" at all: in truth, it was within my parents' power to go to *Eretz Yisrael*, if not so easily during the years of the British Mandate, then certainly after the establishment of the state. They declined to do so, and *chose* to go to Canada instead when presented with the opportunity. My mother's story about families with infants being turned away during the War of Independence was not a deliberate falsification, but rather a guilt-assuaging rationalization by someone who, to this day, has not made peace with her geographical destiny. My mother continues to be haunted by the image of her revered father, the tragic hero who had guided so many others to sanctuary in *Eretz Yisrael* but did not succeed in doing the same for his own family. She understood his dramatic but futile last-minute gesture of registering the entire family as card-carrying members of the Zionist Organization as an ethical will that she was honor-bound to discharge.

The truth is that the members of my family who ended up in Canada had been divided on whether or not to go to Israel. My mother may have wanted desperately to go, but my father craved peace and quiet, which the newborn State of Israel was not in a position to offer him. Dezso the romantic found the idea of *aliya* (immigrating to Israel) alluring, but Vera dreamed of America and all it offered a young orphan refugee. Béla Zimmerman, the idealistic man of letters, was perfectly happy to join his three brothers who were already in Israel. As it turned out, the Canadian fur commission rejected him, making that choice of destination for him. However, Magdi was so disconsolate about this that the Zimmerman family ended up joining the others in Toronto at the first opportunity, twelve years later. Kicsi may have been an impassioned Zionist, longing to join her two sisters in Israel, but Sanyi, after his harrowing experiences in the Mauthausen concentration camp, was afraid of arriving in a country at war. He was to prove his mettle in other ways, in a different time and place.

Some time ago, a number of people around the world e-mailed me a recently discovered BBC recording of survivors of the Bergen-Belsen concentration camp. It is moving to hear them sing *Hatikva*, the Zionist anthem, at *Shabbos* services on April 20, 1945, following their liberation by British troops. According to the BBC announcer, the open-air services were held in the midst of the camp by the Jewish chaplain to the British Second Army, the Reverend Lawrence H. Hartman.

Could this have been the very same Rabbi "Laurenzio" Hartman who, we learned earlier, had performed weddings at the British-administered Grugliasco displaced persons' camp, including, presumably, that of my own parents? This individual was clearly an Englishman serving his country, not a "religious Zionist fellow refugee from Yugoslavia awaiting his turn to go to Palestine", as my mother reported her officiating rabbi to be. Was there a different person, fitting this description, whose name was somehow omitted from the Jewish community records? Or, was my mother confused about the identity of the rabbi who performed her wedding, as she had been confused regarding "Professor Doctor Levi" performing my circumcision? Nothing seems quite so certain anymore.

Dr. Marvin Silverman[1] was finally able to sit down and relax after a long and exhausting day at the hospital in downtown Toronto. Turning on the TV and flipping through the channels, he realized that the Winter Olympic Games were taking place in Torino, Italy. A memory fragment from the remote past flashed into his consciousness.

On an impulse, Dr. Silverman turned to his computer and Googled the words "Torino Jewish community." He quickly arrived at the web site of the *Comunità Ebraica di Torino*, and in the *Contact Us* section, he typed the following query:

> *I was born in a hospital in Torino, Italy on April 6, 1948. My parents were Jewish refugee survivors from Lodz, Poland. How can I retrieve my birth record?*

Anna, the ever-helpful secretary of Chief Rabbi Somekh, was pleased to respond. Not only was it possible to obtain a copy of his birth certificate from City Hall, but the Torino Jewish community also had a detailed record of every circumcision performed on the sons of the refugees. It would be the community's pleasure to share this information with Dr. Silverman. Moreover, he might be interested to know that a young woman in the community had recently completed a dissertation on the Grugliasco displaced persons' camp during the period 1945–1949. If he wished to have further information about her research, he could contact Sara Vinçon directly.

Dr. Silverman immediately sent an e-mail to Sara, telling her how delighted he was to be making this connection and asking whether she might send him a copy of her dissertation. He pointed out that he was not the only child of Grugliasco living in Toronto. A first cousin of his was born in Torino on March 1, 1948, and he had a friend who was born there as well.

Sara responded that, regrettably, her dissertation had not yet been translated into English from the original Italian, which she assumed Dr. Silverman could not read. She was intrigued to learn that there were other Grugliasco babies living in Toronto. In the course of her research, she had encountered one such individual. His parents had spent nearly three years in the camp before immigrating to Canada. These people were now like family to her, and she loved them so much that mere words could not adequately express the depth of her feelings. The mother of the person in question was an especially eloquent and prolific source of information regarding the camp. If Dr. Silverman wished to know more about the experiences of Jewish refugees in the Grugliasco camp, Sara concluded her e-mail, she would be more than happy to put him in touch with these people.

The new turn of events touched Sara profoundly. As she wrote to me at the time:

> *I am REALLY, REALLY moved. I feel as if all the babies I have prayed for while reading their birth certificates are becoming real, like a new family. I already keep all of you close to my heart.*

I was quite moved as well. Dr. Silverman's cousin was a mere four days older than me. His mother must have been in the maternity ward at the same time as my own. She could even have been in the neighboring bed. Here were people whose destiny had intersected with ours during the Italian sojourn, and who had been living like us in Toronto all these years, yet we had never crossed paths.

I sent an e-mail to Dr. Silverman, introducing myself and greeting him as a *landsman* (fellow countryman). I told him that if he wished to know more about the Grugliasco camp, I would be happy to share with him the considerable trove of information I had accumulated on this subject. Like him, I also knew another two Grugliasco babies who had come to Toronto, my cousins Annie Rubinstein Kohn and David Zimmerman. Without even trying, we had already identified six of us, and surely there must be others. *Wouldn't it be wonderful to organize a reunion?*

I received a cordial response from Dr. Silverman. He remarked that his parents never spoke about their time in Grugliasco. His father had passed away several years earlier, and his mother was spending the winter in Florida, as she did every year. He was now determined that when she returned to Toronto in early April, he would sit her down and get her to provide details of her life in the camp.

When I told my mother about the new Grugliasco connection, right here in Toronto, she was very excited. She looked forward to meeting her camp-mate, Mrs. Silverman, and exchanging notes. Even more, she looked forward to meeting her maternity ward-mate, Mrs. Silverman's sister-in-law. With mounting anticipation, she awaited Mrs. Silverman's return from Florida. Finally, she dialed the number that Marvin had provided and left a detailed message.

Two days later, she had received no response. She left another message... and another... and another. Finally, an older woman with a Yiddish accent answered the phone. When my mother introduced herself and asked if she could please speak with Mrs. Silverman, the line went dead.

My mother was quite upset. I promised her I would try to find out what was going on. I phoned Marvin and left a message requesting that he call me back. He never did. Then I sent him the following e-mail:

> *Marvin, I do not know what to make of your unresponsiveness. I hope you are well, and I hope I have not inadvertently given offence. Could you please favor me with the courtesy of a simple answer to the following question, after which I promise never to bother you again:* Do you and your mother have difficulty dealing with and coming to terms with the Grugliasco experience?

The next day, Marvin responded:

> *Yes, my mom has difficulty with her Grugliasco experience, and she is uncomfortable going through this again. Sorry!*

I have kept my promise. In truth, the Silvermans' reactions were consistent with everything I have learned and observed over the years. If no one in my own family, with the exception of my mother, ever talked about Grugliasco, why should Mrs. Silverman be expected to do so?

There are other considerations as well, which underscore the naïveté of fantasizing about an emotional reunion of Grugliasco alumni.

As they moved step by step up the socio-economic ladder, my relatives found themselves increasingly estranged from the others who had arrived with them in Toronto in the fall of 1948. At the very beginning, the refugees who participated in the furriers' project had stayed close. They were bound together by their recent common experience, and they sought solace in one another's company among the not very welcoming strangers in whose midst they found themselves. However, the members of the group gradually drifted apart as their distinctively Canadian realities grew in importance and came to eclipse the shared memories of the refugee camp. Slowly, each individual began to form social bonds with those sharing fundamental affinities. Everyone wished to succeed in the new country; no one wished to remain trapped in the past. In time, the differences always lurking beneath the surface came to overwhelm the increasingly tenuous commonalities. The members of my family were the only Hungarians in the group, the others being mostly of Polish origin. My relatives gradually reintegrated with their Jewish religious heritage, while the others mainly continued to identify with the secular Zionist groups such as Betar and Hashomer Hatzair that had been active in the camps. When the others joined synagogues, these were likely to be Conservative and not Orthodox, so that there was no social interaction between my family and the others on Saturday mornings. As only a very few had a background as furriers, hardly any remained in this field once they had fulfilled their one-year contract with the Canadian government. They either reverted to their original old country occupations, or they sought out one of the many opportunities offered by the post-war economic boom in Toronto.

In March 2004, a memorial service was held in Toronto for the Hungarian Jews murdered by the Nazis, on the occasion of the sixtieth anniversary of the deportations from Hungary. Some survivors of Polish origin objected indignantly. They pointed to the fact that the Nazis only started deporting the Hungarian Jews during the closing months of the War, whereas the Polish Jews had borne the full brunt of genocidal brutality throughout the long years of the German occupation of Poland. "Those people have their nerve," so went the complaint. "*We* are the ones who went through hell. What could *they* possibly know about suffering?"

After only a few years, my parents were completely out of touch with the people who arrived with them at Union Station that crisp September morning in 1948. Whatever bonds once joined them together have long since melted away.

Keeping Faith

It is fall in southern Ontario, and the woods embracing Sunnybrook Hospital are a blaze of autumnal colors. Deceptively vivid are the hues of nature's decay. This morbid thought bears down on me as I enter the oncology ward to visit my cousin Annie. She is undergoing aggressive treatment for the cancer that has come raging back after years of remission. The chemotherapy has been debilitating, and during the past few weeks Annie was unable to receive visitors. I am glad she is prepared to see me now, as I take this to mean she is feeling better.

Annie greets me warmly and surprises me with her opening words. "Eli, I have a lot of time to think in this place, and I've been wondering: How did our parents find the strength to cope with their terrible experiences during the War?

Taken aback, I grope for an appropriate answer. "Well … it seems to me that people really don't know what they are capable of until they are put to the test. Obviously, our parents had what it takes." As I speak, I am thinking of Annie herself no less than of our parents. I have known this remarkable person my entire life, and I understand what is on her mind. She has fought her personal battle with astonishing courage and determination. When she was first diagnosed with cancer twelve years earlier, the doctors told her she had at most three months to live. Annie refused to cooperate in confirming the medical prognosis, as she had too many good reasons to stay alive. She was not ready to leave her devoted childhood-sweetheart husband Tommy and her loving children and grandchildren. Far too much did she cherish her stimulating work, her beautiful homes, her broad circle of friends, her interesting travels around the world, and the many opportunities to touch the lives of others through acts of kindness.

Annie and I have so much in common. We have been cousins, play-mates, schoolmates, neighbors, and business partners our whole lives. Yet, Annie and I are very different people. I am as tall as she is short. I am as quiet and reserved as she is vivacious and outgoing. I am as inclined toward the cerebral as she is grounded in concrete realities.

I had always felt that there was another difference, a particularly significant one, between Annie and me. I had long been conscious of the fact that while both of our fathers were unable to talk about the past, I was blessed with a mother who referred to it frequently, eloquently, and with an all-embracing passion. This immeasurably enriched my sense of connectedness to the tragic history of my family, and rendered it an inte-gral part of my persona. Vera Néni, on the other hand, could never bring herself to discuss her own wartime experiences. The closest Annie's late mother ever came to doing this was to remark on rare occasions: "If you only knew the terrible places I was in, the horrible things I saw during the War! You wouldn't believe it." The particulars were always left to the listener's imagination, and when faced with such a wealth of unpleasant possibilities, the imagination generally chooses to play safe. Since she had grown up in a home where both her parents fell mute regarding the past, I had always assumed that Annie was neither interested in nor informed about it. The fact that we had never discussed such matters throughout all the years seemed to support my assumption.

How mistaken I had been. Having struggled so valiantly against her own mortal enemy, Annie was sensitized to the suffering that our parents had endured, with an immediacy that I could only imagine. Standing in that hospital room, I felt a deep resonance with my cousin, and I thought back to that other hospital, long ago and far away, where the two of us received our humble initiation into a most unpromising world.

Since arriving in Canada as babies, we have been blessed beyond all imagining. I often wonder by what merit it was given to us, the sec-ond generation, to lead such a charmed existence, so sheltered from evil, so utterly removed from the travails of our parents. The untimely death of loved ones has been the ever-present backdrop to my life, but it was always safely isolated in the past. Annie's illness was a rude intrusion into my fool's paradise, a bracing shot of reality.

I know in my heart that despite her courageous determination to survive, the enemy is winning. Annie cannot have much time left, and the worst of her suffering is yet to come. As I contemplate my kindred spirit from Grugliasco lying in her hospital bed, I have never been so conscious of my own mortality.

Over the years, my mother has written extensively about her wartime experiences. Her stories gestated within her for a long time, the emotional turmoil that inspired them gradually transforming into thoughtful coherence. For many years after the terrible events they recalled, there was no audience at hand to hear my mother's stories. People were simply not ready to listen, but in truth, she was not ready to speak either. The passage of time gradually dissolved the communication barrier. When her moment finally arrived, my mother was seized by eloquence quite startling in a woman who had never addressed an audience. Like the rabbis of the Talmud, she had misgivings about imprisoning her dynamic spoken words on static pages. Like the rabbis, she also arrived at the desperate conclusion that if she did not soon ground her memories in text, they would evaporate and be lost forever.

Of all my mother's stories, one in particular has had a remarkable effect on people. Thousands of visitors of all ages and backgrounds at the Holocaust Remembrance Centre in Toronto have been moved to tears by her presentation of the story of the "Five Gold Watches":[1]

> In the late fall of 1944, I was doing forced labor in the Auschwitz concentration camp. Twenty of us young girls formed a team whose job it was to clean the four watchtowers surrounding the crematorium. Five girls were assigned to each tower. On quiet days, when there was little activity in the crematorium, we dared to leave the towers after finishing our work, and went to pick blackberries at the edge of what was called the Forbidden Forest. If we were lucky enough to pick a pailful of berries and smuggle it back into the camp, we could sell it for the ultimate luxury, a whole loaf of bread.
>
> As we emerged from the forest one day, the commandant of the crematorium noticed us. He angrily ordered us to hand our berries

over to him. Before we had a chance to think about the terrible situation we were in, a soldier was behind us, marching us back to the camp at gunpoint. Confused and frightened, we were forced to stand in the main square for a long time, while the Germans considered what to do about us. They reached the verdict that we had wanted to run away, and the punishment for that crime was death by public hanging. They decided that the sentence would be carried out the next morning at 10:00 A.M.

Usually, the entire camp population was forced to watch, so that they might understand the horrible consequences for those who tried to escape. Of the five of us, two had sisters who were not involved in our terrible predicament. They ran about hysterically, pleading for advice on what to do. No one had an answer for them. Since there was no proper trial, there was no opportunity to present a defense. The Germans simply did as they pleased, and nothing could be done about it.

Late that night, one of our supervisors urged us to go over to the next compound and ask for the *Blockelteste*, named Ethel, who had a reputation for being a very kind soul. Although she had been in Auschwitz a very long time, she had not lost her sense of compassion for her fellow human beings. She was responsible for a thousand women, and she always tried to be humane.

When we arrived, she had just lit the Sabbath candle in her little cubicle. She had heard about our misfortune, and she gently told us what we already knew, that there was no way out of our terrible situation. She prayed with us, blessed us, and wished us a peaceful journey. Numb in soul and body, we walked back to our sleeping quarters.

That night was the longest night in my life. Early in the morning, a young girl arrived with a message from Ethel. She had contacted the commandant and negotiated with him. He agreed that for five gold watches, our lives would be spared. The watches were found in no time at all. The sentence was cancelled, with a dire warning never to visit the forest again.

Later, we found out that our German supervisor had co-operated with Ethel in order to save himself. He had been running a business on the side, smuggling liquor to the workers in the crematorium in return for gold, diamonds, and other valuables that were removed from the Jewish victims. He was terrified that the commandant might ask him where he had been while we were wandering around in the forest.

A few weeks later, we were shipped to Germany, where we worked until liberation the next spring. I never heard of Ethel again. I didn't even know what her family name was or where she came from.

Ten years ago, a good friend of mine returned from Israel with the story that a woman from her hometown had become the grandmother of quintuplets. The family was very poor, and it was difficult to raise the five children. My heart went out to them. I started to send money and parcels to this family. Each time, I would receive an appreciative thank-you note from the grandmother. Only when the children were five years old did I find out, from a chance conversation with a fellow survivor, that the grandmother was none other than Ethel, who had saved me from the gallows. Unfortunately, by that time she had passed away. To my everlasting regret, I never had an opportunity to thank Ethel for the gift of life.

Although they sound like fictional characters, the Wechsler quintuplets of Beersheba are real people, now in their late twenties. My mother has a collection of photographs that were sent over the years by their grateful parents, Sarah and Yosef, chronicling the various stages of the children's development. She has never actually met Ethel's grandchildren, although she has been to Israel quite a number of times since making contact with the family. Beersheba was always out of the way, and there was never enough time to go there. Perhaps my mother subconsciously avoided meeting the Wechslers, in order to preserve the epic quality of her remarkable tale.

Implicit in the story of the "Five Gold Watches" is a powerful proclamation of faith. In a depraved world, my mother was able to discover goodness and purpose. Six million other Jews, including those dearest to her, may have been murdered for no apparent reason and without benefit of divine intervention. Yet, my mother is convinced that she and her workmates were saved by a miracle. Furthermore, she believes that she received confirmation of the miracle years later through the unnatural recurrence of the number five. A person of lesser faith might regard my mother's "salvation" as indicative of resourcefulness and a hardy constitution, combined with no small measure of good luck, and the discovery of the quintuplets as a mere interesting coincidence.

My mother could not possibly have written this story in the early years following the War. At Auschwitz, she was able to keep up her spirits and resist the unrelenting attempts to dehumanize her. She did this by maintaining her Jewish consciousness with quiet determination. Observing the dietary laws was out of the question: she never forgot her father's parting exhortation to eat whatever food she was given, so that she might have the physical strength to survive. Nor was it possible to observe *Shabbos* properly, as refusal to work on that day would have meant certain death. She and a few friends chose to focus on small, prudent things. They kept track of *Shabbos* and festivals by scratching a Jewish calendar on the wall in a dark corner of their barracks, and commemorated these special days by devising ersatz candles of margarine and string lit surreptitiously in the middle of the night. During the ominous times when all her energies were consumed by the struggle to survive, my mother's faith was not yet challenged by the cataclysm engulfing the Jewish people. As part of her unwitting strategy to maintain the will to live, she persuaded herself that somehow, the members of her own family must also have escaped death.

It was only after her liberation, when she was no longer preoccupied with the daily struggle to stay alive, that my mother could begin to think about the catastrophe that had befallen her family and her people. She had been raised to believe that as long as Jews fulfilled their duty to God by keeping his Torah, God would, in turn, fulfill his duty to them by protecting them from harm. God had clearly failed to keep his end of the bargain. My mother seethed with pain and anger. At the first *Yizkor* service she attended after the War, she could not bring herself to recite the hallowed words, much as she yearned to honor the memory of her brutally murdered parents and brothers.

My mother's initial impulse was to run far away from the identity that had brought her so much torment. But after a while, she realized that withdrawal brought no satisfaction, only emptiness. She was hurting herself by discarding the Jewish heritage that had always grounded her and imbued her life with meaning.

She reverted to the ways of a traditional Jew, and this reconnected her with her lost family and community. In time, she made peace with God and succeeded in reclaiming her faith. It was only when she reached this point that she could look back at her deliverance from Auschwitz and see the hand of God behind it.

Sadly, though, this was not the norm for survivors. Most were unable to recapture the innocent faith of their youth. Those who could not break away entirely from their religious moorings railed against the God who had forsaken his covenant with the Jewish people. Those more attuned to the prevailing *Zeitgeist* simply concluded that God did not exist. The unrestrained murder of six million Jews served to erode faith in divine providence and accelerated the long-term process of religious attrition characteristic of the modern period.

Sara Vinçon was blessed with a sharp eye for detail, a most useful attribute in a student of history. The first question she asked me, at the beginning of our e-mail correspondence, was whether I could explain the discrepancy between the notation in my birth certificate that I was born at 19:00 and the notation in the community circumcision registry that I was born at 17:00. I responded confidently that 17:00 must have been the correct time. Why so? March 5, 1948, I pointed out, was a Friday, and my perpetual worldwide Jewish calendar informed me that *Shabbos* candle lighting in Torino that day would have been a few minutes before 18:00. Jewish law required that if I was born before candle-lighting time, my circumcision had to take place eight days later, on the following Friday. Were the birth certificate time of 19:00 correct, resulting in a *Shabbos* birth and a Saturday morning *bris*, my family would not have been able to travel from Grugliasco to Torino for the happy event. The community registry must be correct regarding the time of my birth, but mistaken in claiming that my *bris* took place on Saturday, which was March 13, not 12.

I was pleased with myself for demonstrating such forensic acuity, but something about the discrepancy troubled me. I needed confirmation from those who had been present at the circumcision ceremony. Unfortunately, the ranks of the Grugliasco veterans were by now severely depleted. Béla Zimmerman, Vera Rubinstein, and Kicsi Hofstedter had all passed away. Danny Rubinstein was afflicted with dementia. Magdi

Zimmerman, like my father, refused to talk about the past, and, in any event, claimed not to remember anything. My mother, the usually dependable and forthcoming family historian, had not been present at the *bris*. In keeping with the practice of the time, women in the Maria Vittoria maternity ward were confined to two weeks of strict bed-rest as if they were recovering from a serious illness, and circumcisions were performed well out of their delicate sight elsewhere in the hospital.

That left only Sandy Hofstedter.

One *Shabbos* morning, I found myself walking home from *shul* with Sandy. I asked him if he remembered whether my *bris* had taken place on a Friday or a Saturday. "No," he answered. "Who can remember such things after so many years? What does it matter, anyway?" I explained that the notation in the Torino Jewish community register indicating that the bris was on *Shabbos* troubled me. The family would not have been able to travel from Grugliasco to be there that day, but I know that everyone came. Sandy laughed. "What are you talking about? Nobody cared in those days. It made no difference if it was Friday or Saturday."

I should not have been surprised by his response, for in truth, Sandy was not telling me anything I did not already know. Although I did not often stop to think about it, I was aware that our elders had returned to the Judaism of their youth after a period of tormented alienation. I knew this from adult-era retrospection upon disjointed, incompletely processed childhood memories. This knowledge has been augmented by sporadic documentary evidence such as Sandy's remarkably frank oral testimony published in a family chronicle:

> Nobody thought very much about Jewish life or religion... You have to understand that, after the war, we were all very much confused. The whole family was very religious before but, afterwards, everybody kept asking the same questions. They were very difficult times. It took some people years to get back on the right track. We are very thankful that we got back ourselves. Many people, unfortunately, never regained their faith in religion.[2]

Still, I was taken aback by Sandy's admirable candor, which compelled me to face up to my own inadvertent lack of it. It was not a deliberate prevarication: rather, so malleable is human memory that I had read my family's present high level of Jewish observance into the past without even realizing it.

Surprising complexities occasionally burst forth amid the contrived simplicity of my parents' spiritual world. Some years ago, my father confided to me that he had difficulty believing in the coming of the Messiah. As far as he was concerned, if God did not send *Mashiach* at the time of his people's most desperate need, there was no rationale for continuing to await his arrival. My father was a bright and perceptive person whose wisdom came not from reading books, but from living life, and the notion of a miraculous redeemer of the Jewish people clashed gratingly with his personal experience. He was well aware that he was challenging a core principle of Judaism, and his heterodoxy troubled him. Yet, he had to be true to himself. He was defiant on this point, despite his unwavering devotion to the traditional Jewish way of life.

It would appear that such an eclectic blend of rebellious thought and faithful practice is quite common among observant survivors.

During a recent family gathering, someone expressed the pious wish that a certain gravely ill neighbor might be granted a *yeshua,* a heavenly salvation. The reaction of an ostensibly devout survivor startled those present: "I don't believe in miracles. After our people were murdered, and God didn't do anything to stop it, there is no reason to count on him now. We have to help ourselves." Every survivor knows that in the camps one could not rely on miracles. Those who lived by their wits and worked diligently had at least a chance of staying alive. Those who sat back and waited for divine intervention had no chance whatsoever.

It would seem that believing is one thing, and having faith is another. For the minority of survivors who returned to a religious way of life, a certain skepticism was inevitable. These people had seen too much to remain simple believers. Faith, however, is a different matter, as it facilitates carrying on in the world and staking a claim on the future.

My thoughts wander back to Torino. A number of years ago, the pedestrian mall in front of the Tempio Israelitico was renamed "*Piazzetta Primo Levi*" in honor of the Jewish community's most famous son. I remember standing there and gazing up at the august twin-towered house of worship. Rather a curious spot, it struck me, to commemorate someone who was a principled atheist. I felt a certain affinity with this man who was born in Torino just like me, and who was an inmate of Auschwitz with a number on his forearm and a compulsion to bear witness, just like my mother. Then I recalled that this uncommonly gifted and sensitive human being failed to subdue his personal demons, with tragic consequences. He struggled for years against severe bouts of depression, finally succumbing to his suicidal impulses. As a writer, Judith Rubinstein cannot be mentioned in the same breath as the sublime Primo Levi. Yet as a survivor, she has been far more successful than he. Lacking faith, Primo Levi despaired of the future. Reclaiming her faith, my mother was able to embrace the future.

While conducting research some years ago for a book about the wartime experiences of Toronto-area survivors, a certain local writer was told that he really should meet Mrs. Judith Rubinstein. He arranged an interview, and predictably, he was smitten by the story of the watches and the quintuplets. He requested permission to rework the story in his own words for inclusion in the book. My mother turned him down after reading an early draft. She was upset that someone would take literary liberties with her narrative.

More recently, I received an e-mail from an acquaintance who was excited about a piece that had been spreading like wildfire among ultra-Orthodox Jews around the world, courtesy of the Internet. She was struck by the uncanny resemblance between this story and "Five Gold Watches," and asked that I pass it on to my mother, who would surely find it fascinating.

As soon as I finished reading, I fired off an irate reply to the well-intentioned dispatcher. There was indeed a striking similarity to my mother's story, I pointed out, but not by coincidence: clearly, someone had taken my mother's original and rendered it into a mediocre parody, changing the names to stereotypically Jewish ones and introducing many extraneous, melodramatic, and nonsensical embellishments. The anonymous author obviously considered the original insufficiently pious. But the core theme survived all the literary mutilation. That which made the story so compelling, so magical, was the linkage between Ethel's (or Shaina's, in the revisionist version) saving of the five girls and her being rewarded years later with quintuplet grandchildren.

I did not have the heart to share the news with my mother. Knowing how possessive she was of her story and how sensitive she was to even the most benign tinkering with it, I was sure that this particularly grotesque adaptation would cause her sleepless nights.

In the spring of 2007, my mother attended the Emunah Women of Toronto annual dinner, as she had been doing for many years. The guest speaker was Liebe Geft, the highly regarded director of the Museum of Tolerance in Los Angeles. In the course of her presentation, Mrs. Geft related an inspiring tale she had heard. It concerned five young women who were miraculously saved from death in a concentration camp by a privileged inmate rewarded years later with the birth of quintuplet grandchildren. My mother was beside herself. When the presentation was completed, she went up to the guest speaker and pointed out that the tale was a mangled variant of her own true-life story. Mrs. Geft was surprised and fascinated to learn this.

For my part, I was intrigued by the rapid evolution of my mother's story into a contemporary folk-tale, and so I contacted Liebe Geft on her return home, seeking information. It turned out that she had heard the story from a friend in Miami. It was apparently the same anonymously authored revisionist version that had been e-mailed to me and to a great many other people the previous winter. When Liebe came back to Toronto a short time later, she visited my mother at home and listened intently as she spoke with her customary passion about Auschwitz and about the Wechsler quintuplets.

Several weeks later, Liebe e-mailed me the following message:

I spoke with your mother upon our return to LA, and she gave me the phone number for Sarah Wechsler in Beersheba. I called Sarah and explained the extraordinary sequence of events that led me to her. She confirmed the details about the quintuplets and the generous support and assistance your mother has provided, but she denied any connection with events in Auschwitz. Her mother, Ethel Wald, came to Israel in 1939 and did not suffer imprisonment during the Shoah. Clearly, this Ethel is not the same lady as the person who your mother believes helped save her and the other four girls from death in Auschwitz.

145

I was in turmoil. The linkage between the deliverance of the five women from certain death and the birth of quintuplets to the daughter of their savior turned out to be either a misunderstanding or a fabrication! However, once I was able to ponder the matter dispassionately, I realized that what my mother wrought in devising the linkage was perfectly in character for her. Yet again, as she had done countless times since the end of the War, she was imposing purposefulness on a world that seemed utterly devoid of it. This empowered her to reclaim her humanity.

I have come to understand that the survivors who were able to reconstruct their lives successfully were those who were resourceful in conjuring up positive new realities. Their dreadful experiences during the War had pushed them toward the conclusion that evil reigned victorious in the world. However, accepting this as a fact would cause them to despair of the future. Thus, they compelled themselves to see goodness and light even where, objectively speaking, none was present.

In a later e-mail, Liebe Geft offered a thoughtful reflection:

> *It certainly makes sense, given the information provided to your mother that Ethel was the name of the quintuplets' grandmother, that the serendipity seemed fateful and your mother accepted it without further inquiry. As far as I am concerned, there are two separate stories: 1) what happened in Auschwitz – and I believe your mother's version is true and accurate. And unrelated to that, 2) your mother's extraordinary generosity in coming to the aid of a needy family in Israel, whom she did not know and never met. It does not detract from this wonderful, spontaneous* mitzvah *that, years later, she learned that the grandmother of these children was a woman from Hungary, by the name of Ethel, who survived/escaped the Shoah, and the association with what had happened in Auschwitz evoked feelings of gratitude. In the first story, your mother was one of five souls saved in Auschwitz. Later, in the second story, in a very real way, it was your mother who helped save 'five souls'. For me, she is the true hero.*

The Feast of Perfect Faith

Hard work and personal sacrifice, combined with no small measure of good fortune, enabled my parents gradually to reconstruct their shattered lives in Canada. They achieved material comfort and security, and became respected members of the community. They remained, throughout the years, what they had always been, decent and well-balanced human beings beloved by all who knew them.

However, there were vestiges of past horrors that simply refused to fade away. My father would suffer from anxiety whenever he encountered an official in uniform or saw a large dog in the street. He knew it was irrational, but he could not help it.

My mother, for her part, continued to experience distress whenever she encountered people speaking German, or when she heard the siren of an emergency vehicle screaming by.

There is something particularly inscrutable about air travel, a mode of transportation my parents first experienced only after the difficult early years had passed. Over and over again, airplanes have provided a flash point for the unpleasant intrusion of the past into their present.

In April of 1974, my father was returning from the joyous dinner celebrating my engagement to Renée in New York. My mother had decided to stay on for several days to visit with relatives, but, as always, my father was eager to get back to work in Toronto. My mother asked him to take home her necklace and earrings. Worried that he would be late for his flight, he absent-mindedly thrust the jewelry into the pocket of his jacket and rushed off.

Upon his arrival at Pearson Airport in Toronto, my father had to clear Canadian immigration and customs. When he reached the front of the line and saw the official in his military-style uniform and cap, he broke out in a cold sweat. The routine questions – *Where do you live? What was the purpose of your visit to the United States?* – evoked nervous, stammering responses. The official naturally reacted to the "nothing to declare" entry on the customs form with suspicion. My father was searched thoroughly along with his luggage. Sure enough, there in his jacket pocket was the jewelry. His protests that it had been purchased in Toronto years earlier, and that he was simply taking it home at his wife's request, were to no avail. By now, my poor father was totally beside himself. They finally let him go, but without the jewelry. The next day, his jeweler corroborated that the items in question had indeed been purchased in Canada, and customs promptly released them. My father remained deeply troubled by the experience. From that day on, every border crossing was a painful ordeal for him.

Years later, on the evening of January 16, 1991, I boarded a flight to Frankfurt, on my way to business meetings in Munich. When the plane landed in Frankfurt, I learned that while we were in the air, the United States had launched a massive bombing offensive against Iraq. The airport was thick with German soldiers, in response to threats of terrorist attacks. I continued on to Munich, checked into the hotel, and went to the first of my meetings.

That night, at 3:00 A.M., I was roused from a deep sleep by the ringing of the telephone. It was Renée calling from Toronto.

"Eli, were you sleeping?"

"Of course I was. It's 3:00 in the morning!"

"How can you be sleeping? Don't you know what's going on?"

"Sure I do. The Americans are finally bombing the daylights out of Iraq, just as they have been threatening to do for months."

"Here's your mother. She wants to talk to you."

I barely recognized my mother's voice. She was crying hysterically. "Eli, the Germans are killing our people again! What are you doing there? Come home; please come home, right away!"

I was shocked to hear my usually unflappable mother so distraught, and I was mystified by what she was saying. What did the Germans have to do with this? Renée came on the line again: "Eli, haven't you heard that the Iraqis are firing missiles with chemical warheads at Israel?"

Now I understood. The media reported earlier that Saddam Hussein had acquired chemicals from German firms that could be used in his Scud missiles. He was threatening to fire these at Israel in the event Iraq was attacked by the United States. Soon after the start of the war, he delivered on his promise. In the early hours, it was reported (incorrectly, as it turned out) that the Scuds were fitted with chemical warheads. It all came together in a totally irrational, yet from my mother's point of view, compelling manner. The Jews were being killed by their enemies. They were being killed with poison gas, just as they had been during the Second World War. The poison gas was German. Her son was in Germany. Ergo, once again Germans were killing her family.

Then my daughter Tamar came on the line, unnerved by her grandmother's uncharacteristic outburst. "Abba, please come home right away!" she sobbed. "Everyone is going crazy here. They told us in school today that terrorists are trying to attack Jews everywhere, and we had armed policemen guarding the school building. All the kids were crying their heads off. And Grandma is really scary. I've never seen her like this. You should be here with the family, Abba. We need you!"

What could I do? The women in my life were ordering me home. It was absurd: I had just arrived in Munich, and I had work to do. Worst of all, it was early Friday morning, and I did not have a reservation back to Toronto at a time of war. On principle, I always try to avoid traveling on Fridays, especially over long distances, lest I find myself violating *Shabbos*.

I hastily packed my bag, checked out of the hotel, grabbed a cab to the airport, and got on the next shuttle flight to Frankfurt. I arrived to a scene of pandemonium, with an even heavier military presence than the day before, augmented by attack dogs. Passengers were trapped in endless queues. After security personnel interrogated me at length, turned my bags inside out, and confiscated my electric shaver, I was allowed to rebook my flight, check in, and wait with all the other anxious passengers for boarding to commence. One delay was followed by another, and another. When we were finally allowed onto the plane, I figured I would arrive in Toronto a mere half hour before sundown, too close for comfort. But there was no turning back now. Sure enough, once we taxied for take-off, there was a further delay of half an hour. At this point, I could not get off the plane. All the way to Toronto, I had visions of walking home from the airport for several hours along the highway, in the dark freezing cold.

Upon arrival at Pearson Airport, I was dumbfounded to see Renée waiting for me at the gate. I was certainly happy to see her, but I felt badly that she would have to endure the long frigid walk as well. I should have known better: my ever-resourceful wife had reserved a room at a hotel across the road, and stocked it with candles, wine, *challot*, and home-cooked delicacies. Renée and I collapsed into a special *Shabbos* experience as stranded wayfarers in our own town. All that day, I kept thinking about how my parents' unwavering devotion to the *Shabbos* had given them strength to return from the abyss. I also thought long and hard about my mother's disturbing display of fragility and what had brought it on.

My father voluntarily stopped driving at ninety because he no longer trusted his reflexes. However, he continued to attend synagogue services early each morning, work half a day at the office, and swim vigorously in the afternoon. Every day, he tracked his stock portfolio and read the newspaper from cover to cover, evincing a vivid awareness of the world around him.

Everything changed shortly before his ninety-fourth birthday.

Our son Ilan was getting married to Dana, a wonderful young woman in New York. With joyous hearts, the entire family prepared to fly to New York for the wedding.

My father had not flown anywhere in several years, and much as he wanted to share in the family's special moment, he dreaded the trip. Aside from his discomfort with uniformed officials, he had always been a reluctant traveler. As he saw it, the circumstances of his tumultuous past had compelled him to do a great deal of traveling against his will. Now that he was finally in control of his life, he took pleasure in choosing freely to stay at home.

Yet, he knew that on this particular occasion, he simply *had* to fly to New York. There was a time many years before when he could not imagine having children of his own, much less grandchildren. *Granted the precious opportunity to dance at a grandchild's wedding, how could he not be there?*

We did everything in our power to make the trip as easy and as stress-free as possible. My father did not have to worry about a thing – yet worry he did. *Would the flight be on time? What if we got stuck in traffic on the way to the airport? What if the weather took a turn for the worse? What if the luggage got lost and he didn't have his good suit to wear?*

Once safely delivered to the wedding, my father seemed to be fine. He reveled in the role of family patriarch, drawing untold pleasure from his children, grandchildren, and great-grandchildren. He astonished everyone including himself by staying until the very end, well past midnight, savoring every moment.

We failed to persuade him to stay on with us in New York, to enjoy some quiet family time after all the excitement. The wedding was over, and he wanted to get back home as soon as possible. Rochelle was to accompany our parents on the flight back to Toronto at noon on the day after the wedding.

My father was fully packed, dressed, and ready to go at 4:00 a.m. He was worried that he would miss the flight. My poor mother, exhausted from the intensity of the last few days and no youngster herself, pleaded with him in vain to get back to bed.

When we saw him later on, we were very disturbed. He had never been like this before – fearful and fragile. He was obviously struggling with something deep inside his psyche, and he appeared to be losing the battle.

The trip back to Toronto was a horror. After that, things were never to be the same.

The geriatric psychiatrist prescribed a series of anti-depressants, each in turn more calamitous in its effects than the one before. My father began to hallucinate. All night long, he would pace furiously around the house. He refused to lie down on his bed, believing that if he did, the bed would swallow him up. Convinced that the refrigerator was going to explode, he avoided the kitchen. With terror in his eyes, he muttered incessantly about some unspecified "danger" threatening the family.

The doctors could not say with certainty what was wrong with my father. Perhaps he had suffered a mild stroke that affected the area of his

brain controlling anxiety. They did conclude, however, that he was defi-
nitely not depressed, and so they began to experiment with anti-psychot-
ics. After an agonizing process of trial and error, they finally settled on
one particular drug, which proved effective in relieving the anxiety. The
problem was that it was *too* effective, making my father so drowsy that
he ended up sleeping most of the time – day and night. His well-honed
survival instincts told him that nothing could be worse than not being in
control of himself. And so, he refused to take enough of the medication
to be of therapeutic value, preferring conscious torment to unconscious
oblivion.

The cruelest blow to this dignified man, who had always placed the
highest premium on independence and self-sufficiency, was his sudden
reliance upon strangers for help with his most basic needs. He protested
vehemently when told that he required full-time caregivers if he wished
to continue living in his beloved home on the edge of the wooded ravine. Grudgingly, he conceded the point when Rochelle, Renée, and I
convinced him that the alternative was to transfer him to a senior care
facility.

Of course, my mother could not possibly have been left unaffect-
ed by these troubling changes. Although she was twelve years younger
than her husband, (a common situation among people of their particular
background,) she was certainly old enough in her own right. She often
marveled at the resilience and fortitude she had demonstrated years before when cast into extreme situations. She had never imagined, during
her rather unexceptional childhood, that she possessed such reserves of
strength. But human beings are not built to last forever, and my mother
had recently struggled with her own health problems, including removal
of a malignant tumor and subsequent chemotherapy. As if this were not
enough, she now had to serve as nurturer to a husband radically transformed from the strong, supportive man she had always known. This
highly functioning, positively thinking woman began to show troubling
signs of the depression for which her husband had initially been misdi-
agnosed.

My father had always been a disciplined and punctual person, but
lately he was developing an exaggerated craving for regularity in his
life. Each week, his sense of dread mounted day by day as *Shabbos* approached. This day is unlike any other in its character and rhythms,

normally enabling it to be a source of profound inner peace for the observant Jew, an anchor of stability in a tempestuous world. In my father's case, *Shabbos* was transformed into an oppressive master, tyrannizing the rest of the week. By Friday afternoon, he would be in a state of full-blown panic: *How would he get dressed in his* Shabbos *clothes? Would the timer controlling the lights work properly? Would he remember the words to the prayers? Would there be enough wine for the* Kiddush*, and would he be able to recite it?* It had always been extremely important to him to attend synagogue services, and over the years, he did so with devoted regularity. Now he was terrified of crowds and extremely self-conscious about how he appeared to others, so much that he could no longer bring himself to go to *shul*. He was disappointed in himself over this lapse. By the time the *Havdalah* service came around, marking the end of yet another *Shabbos*, both of my parents were exhausted and disconsolate.

My mother came to dread the arrival of *Shabbos* almost as much as my father did. The cycle repeated itself relentlessly week after week, feeding on itself and generating an unbearable tension in my parents' home.

My father lost interest in practically everything and became a virtual recluse. It took a great deal of coaxing just to get him outdoors for a bit of fresh air. A simple visit to the barber or the doctor became an anxiety-fraught expedition. He was willing to see only close family members, and he declined to receive the many people who would have wished to visit him at home.

Two individuals with whom my father enjoyed a unique rapport because of their congruent pasts were his nieces, Magdi and Borika. As a way of distracting him during these difficult days, they would engage him in conversation, gently nudging him to recollect events and personalities from his old life. As my father had never been willing to speak to me about his past, I was surprised that he would open up in this way to my cousins. Of course, I was curious to know what he told them, but at the same time, I was in dread of uncovering his secrets. I felt it would be a sort of indecent exposure, a violation of filial respect, and so I never questioned Magdi and Borika about their conversations with my father.

There was a time, long ago, when my father was not at all certain that life was worth living. Slowly, he groped his way back from the verge of despair, devoting the ensuing decades to a defiantly ardent affirmation of life. Now, his victory decisively established, my father was no longer able to enjoy the fruits of this victory. As he approached his centenary, he felt that perhaps he had overstayed his welcome in this world. Almost all of his contemporaries, the people best able to understand him, were gone, having died years earlier from the effects of old age. His sole surviving kindred spirit was his "baby" brother Danny, who was two and a half years his junior. Their entire lives, through good times and bad, the Rubinstein brothers had done everything together. With their white hair, ruddy complexions, and sharply defined features, the two brothers bore a striking fraternal resemblance, and people often mistook them for one another. Yet appearances can be deceiving: the glint in Danny's blue eyes and the winning smile were still there, but his mind was long gone, ravaged by dementia. Seeing his brother in this condition upset my father greatly, and only served to remind him of his ever-growing solitude.

After the murder of six million European Jews, only about three million were still alive in 1945. Approximately twenty-five thousand of this number came to Canada, and of these, about twelve thousand are still alive in Toronto. For this reason, Toronto is an ideal laboratory for the study of the unique psychological disorders affecting survivors. As they suffer the infirmities of old age in their waning years, these disorders become increasingly pronounced. The Baycrest Centre for Geriatric Care, the pride and joy of Toronto's Jewish community, has conducted studies and developed special programs for its many residents who are survivors. The staff have been trained to know which stimuli trigger unpleasant memories and are thus to be avoided: showers, bathtubs, white lab coats, the smells of antiseptics, feces, and urine, rigid routines and schedules, darkness, the sounds of people crying or screaming. They have also learned to understand phenomena such as the idiosyncratic need of some residents to hide or hoard food.

My parents continued living in their own home, reconciled to the need for round-the-clock help. My mother had a very difficult year, beginning with knee replacement surgery and culminating in two dislocated shoulders after a fall at home. Following a lengthy stay in the hospital and the rehabilitation centre, she now goes several times a week to the Baycrest Centre for physiotherapy. She goes for the company of her fellow survivors, and does her water exercises on the side. More and more, she talks about the past, her childhood, the War, Italy, and the early years in

Canada. I have heard all the stories many times over, but once in a while, I am startled by something I do not recall having heard before. *Is this perhaps a hoary memory stored in a far recess of her brain and suddenly rising to conscious expression? Or is her aging gray matter no longer replacing itself efficiently, so that she is deceived into recollecting things that never happened?*

The radical cosmetic treatment my father received in the munitions plant in wartime Hungary had still not worn off. The skin on his face was smooth and pink. Although his balance was somewhat uncertain, his heart was strong and his appetite keen. Yet, my father considered his excellent state of health relative to his age a cruel taunt rather than a blessing. When people complimented him on how well he looked for his age, he insisted that the way he looked did not at all reflect the way he felt. His restless mind granted him no serenity. On balance, his life had been good, but he believed that by right, he should have taken his leave long ago like all the others. He felt trapped in a time and place to which he did not belong.

By the end of each week, my father's anxiety would rise to an unbearable crescendo. I tried to be with my parents at the conclusion of *Shabbos* whenever I could, so that I might help navigate through the crisis. My father and I would recite the afternoon *Minchah* prayers, followed by *Seudah Shlishis,* the last of the three traditional *Shabbos* meals. Sitting at the head of the table, my father would occasionally lean over and whisper to me that he was having a panic attack. I start singing the *Askinu Seudasa,* and he haltingly joins in. Soon the tension melts away.

Prepare the feast of perfect faith, the joy of the Holy King. Prepare the feast of the King.

With a faraway look in his eyes, my father chants the ancient melody. It is the same melody he learned from his own father very long ago in Szentistvan, and which has been passed down through innumerable generations of his family. For the moment, my father is transfixed by an extraordinary calmness. He clasps my hand with both of his own. His hands are usually cold, but now they are warm. I feel an intense closeness to him, yet I know he is in a far-away dimension, one that I can never hope to enter.

We proceed to the celebrated Twenty Third Psalm, repeated three times in accordance with the mystical tradition, each time with a different melody. The fingers of my father's right hand, keeping count lest we re-peat too many times, betray the only hint of anxiety.

A Psalm of David: The Lord is my shepherd. I lack for nothing.

We finish, and my father returns abruptly to his present reality. There are plenty of things to worry about: Far too much food is sitting on the table. *Who is going to eat it all before it spoils? And, if it spoils, what would there be to eat tomorrow? Should he have a glass of water, or will this give him an upset stomach?* It is already starting to turn dark, and soon *Shabbos* will be over. We must hurry and recite the grace after meals right away, or else we shall not have enough time for the evening prayers, and then we must immediately perform the *Havdalah* service ending the *Shabbos*. Are we going to have enough wine, did the spices lose their aroma, is the candle going to burn down to nothing, do we have matches? Although the *Havdalah* has formed an integral part of his weekly rhythm for close to a century, my father has lost his self-confidence and reacts agitatedly to the gentle suggestion that he might lead the service now. He insists that I take his place. He is far away, moaning and quivering.

For the Jews there was light, gladness, joy, and honor; so may it be for us.

Tears roll down my mother's cheeks as she smells the sweet spices. All the while, her gaze is fixed on the kitchen wall, adorned with photo-graphs of her grandchildren and great-grandchildren. The service ends, and we wish one another *a gute voch, a gezinte voch, a mazeldike voch* – a good week, a healthful week, a lucky week. My mother raises an arm as high as her recently dislocated shoulder will permit and gestures toward the picture-wall. This, she softly tells my father, is what has made it all worthwhile. We must never stop counting our blessings.

Onward

The phone rang early in the morning. It was Renée calling from Toronto, just as I was opening my eyes in Tel Aviv. I looked at the clock and reflexively subtracted seven hours from the local time.

"Hi, Renée. What are you doing up so late?"

"I'm really sorry, Eli, but I have bad news. Dad suffered a severe stroke, and he is in the emergency ward at Sunnybrook Hospital. We are all here with him. The doctors can't stop the hemorrhaging in his brain. They aren't making predictions, but it doesn't look good. You'd better come home right away."

For years, I had been in dread of something like this happening. Of course, I knew it was only a matter of time. At almost ninety-nine, my father was a very old man, and no one lives forever. But a loving child is never ready for the death of a beloved parent. Moreover, always lurking malevolently at the threshold of my consciousness have been the twin anxieties of air travel and *Shabbos*, holding me hostage to my father's tormented past.

Sure enough, when the call came, it was a Friday, and I was halfway around the world. I grabbed my passport, hailed a cab, and rushed off to Ben Gurion Airport. Air Canada had a direct flight to Toronto scheduled to arrive two hours before *Shabbos*. As a frequent traveler on this route, I was able to plead my way onto the last seat on the plane. Thank God, the twelve-hour flight was uneventful, departing on time and arriving on time. I charged out of the terminal and took a cab across town to the hospital. Rochelle and Renée were there, and true to form, Renée had prepared wine for *Kiddush* and traditional *Shabbos* meals.

157

I grasped my father's unparalyzed left hand, and I was sure I felt him pressing back ever so faintly. His left eye was partially open. Although he was incapable of expressing himself, I sensed that he was aware of my presence.

By the following morning, he had lapsed into a coma. In the afternoon, holding his limp but warm hand, I half sang and half cried *Askinu Seudasa* in his presence one last time.

It was the height of the summer travel season, and all of Bill Rubinstein's progeny – children, grandchildren, and great-grandchildren – were in Toronto. Perhaps my father, ever considerate of others, intuited that this would be a minimally inconvenient time for him to take his leave. We gathered round the bed of the family patriarch in a loving, reverent vigil and awaited the inevitable.

The *levaya,* the traditional funeral service for the one-time refugee fur-worker, who knew not a soul in Toronto when he arrived fifty-nine years earlier, was attended by a remarkably diverse range of people.

During the *Shiva* week of mourning, a constant stream of visitors came through my parents' home, from early in the morning until late at night. No one had to struggle to find the right words.

Mr. Rubinstein was always a perfect gentleman.

Your dad was a person of exceptional integrity in all his dealings.

I loved him as I did my own father, said more than one long-time employee.

I shall never forget how he helped me in my moment of need, without fanfare and with quiet dignity.

Everyone knew Mr. Rubinstein was a man of substance, but he was so modest that he never acted the part.

He treated every human being with respect, even at the end when he was not well.

My nephew Zeke summed it up succinctly in his eulogy: *Grandpa was a real mensch.*

For a long time, I have felt that there is a book lodged deep within me, yearning to break out. When I finally resolved to liberate this book by committing it to text, the process dragged on for several years. Rationalizations were easy enough to find:

I am not really a writer.

My busy life-style does not allow me to focus properly on the demanding task of writing.

Perhaps in the summer things will be quieter.

The truth, I now realize, is that the book languished because deep down, I sensed that my parents' story was incomplete. My mother's narrative is, to be sure, well developed and eloquently articulated. As long as my father was alive, I sustained the hope that someday, somehow, his untold story would come surging forth. Now that he is gone and the hope has been forever extinguished, I am finally at peace.

The months have flashed by since my father's death, and soon the traditional year of mourning will come to an end. I have tried my best to participate regularly in a *minyan*, a quorum of at least ten adult Jewish males, for the three daily prayer services, in order to recite the *Kaddish* for my father as many times as possible. This routine dominates my life, especially when I am traveling, but that would appear to be precisely the intention. The relentless preoccupation with prayer schedules, together with the avoidance of all entertainment and celebratory events during the year of mourning, serve as an ever-present reminder that my father is no longer among us. Every day, I think about the facile, eager fluency with which I utter the ancient Aramaic words of the *Kaddish*. I also think about my mother's anguished *cri de coeur* after Liberation, when she found herself incapable of sanctifying the memory of her murdered parents by attending *Yizkor* services.

In the last few years, both of my parents frequently remarked that they never expected to survive the War, let alone live to an advanced age. When the madness finally subsided, they were amazed that they were still alive, while sorely distressed that most of those dearest to them had been murdered. As the days accumulated into years and the years into decades, my parents slowly learned to rejoice in the bonus gift of life granted to them, and to find profound meaning in it.

Conscious as I am of my parents' tragic past, I often think about the striking contrast between my own life and theirs. What did I ever do to deserve this abundance of all things good, supported by the most wonderful wife, children, and grandchildren? Clearly, it has nothing to do with a surfeit of merit on my part, just as the terrible fate of the Jews of Europe had nothing to do with a dearth of merit on theirs. I am simply fortunate to have been born in the middle of the twentieth century rather than at its beginning.

It is not within our power to choose the circumstances of our earthly sojourn. But as human beings, created in the divine image, we are granted the freedom to make the best we can of these circumstances, whatever they might be. This vital lesson I have learned from my beloved parents, and endeavored to pass on to my own children.

When it came time to order the *matzevah*, the tombstone marking our father's grave, Rochelle and I sought inspiration in the photograph I had once taken of our grandfather Mordechai's *matzevah* in the Mezokovesd cemetery. Of all the family members on both sides who perished during the War, he was the only one to receive a proper Jewish burial, as he had the good fortune to die of old age before the Nazis could deport him to Auschwitz. We decided that it would be a fitting tribute to our father's memory for the *matzevah* of Dov the son of Mordechai to be modeled as faithfully as possible on that of Mordechai the son of Dov. Making a few changes, we replicated the austere and unadorned Hebrew text, so characteristic of the down-to-earth Jews who once inhabited the agricultural hinterland of prewar Hungary. With her artist's sensibility, Rochelle even matched the profile and the dark gray color of the original granite slab.

פ"נ
איש ירא שמים מעודן
בתת רגליו לעבודת בוראו
בנחת רוח קיבל כל אדם
אהב משפחתו בגופו ומהותו

דוב ע"ה
בן מרדכי ע"ה
ושם אמו רבקה ע"ה
שנספה בשואה עק"ה

נפטר ו' אלול ה' תשס"ז

ת נ צ ב ה

Here lies

a gentle, God-fearing man

who hastened to serve his Creator.

He treated everyone with respect,

and loved his family body and soul.

Dov

son of Mordechai.

His mother was Rivka,

who perished in the Holocaust

al kiddush hashem.[1]

Passed away 6 Elul, 5767[2]

May his soul be bound up

in the bundle of life.

After consulting our mother and receiving her whole-hearted approval, Rochelle and I added the following words on the reverse of the tombstone:

In memory of his first family,

wife Ibi and sons

Uri and Mordechai,

who perished in the Holocaust

al kiddush hashem.

Appendix A

The following is the feature article by Gino Li Veli published in the April 15, 1994, edition of La Repubblica, *translated from the Italian by the author.*

Here From Canada To Say "Thank You"
Hungarian Jewess returns to Grugliasco,
where she lived for three years after the lager

After 48 years, she returned to Italy to revisit those places where her life was reconciled following the atrocities she suffered in the concentration camps. So, it was that Judith Rubinstein, a 74-year-old Hungarian Jewess who had immigrated to Canada in 1948, knocked that afternoon on the door of the old psychiatric hospital of Grugliasco. To the astonishment of the doctors and nurses within, she proclaimed that she wished to thank the Italian people for their compassion. The perplexity lasted about ten minutes, and then came the clarification.

Judith Rubinstein was not mistaken: thousands of survivors of the Nazi lagers were accommodated in these buildings for several years after the war. Enveloped by the affection and compassion of the inhabitants of Grugliasco, refugees from all over Europe reclaimed their connection with the world. Judith Rubinstein's story is representative. In Grugliasco, she married her husband. Her son, who with his wife was accompanying her on this adventuresome journey, was born in March 1948 at the Maria Vittoria Hospital on via Cibrario. "There wasn't much to eat," recalls the lady, "but what little there was, the Italians shared with us. For us, this was very important. We have returned to express our appreciation."

But what accounts for the rapport between Judith Rubinstein and Piedmont that the lady wished to renew after such a long time? Returning to Hungary after the tragic experience of Auschwitz, the young Jewess thought she had lost everything, her house, her family. Alone and desperate, she searched for help. She found it at the Red Cross and at UNRRA, a humanitarian organization that made it possible for refugees to overcome many difficulties and emigrate to the West. In March 1946, she arrived with many other escapees in Milano, and several weeks later in Grugliasco.

In the psychiatric institution, which had been transformed during the War into an English military hospital, they were very hospitable to the survivors of the lager. The record of those years is firmly anchored in the lady's memory. "Every week, several thousand arrived. " They were all in desperate straits," she says, "but the Torinese gave them a great deal of help." They even gave Judith Rubinstein a job. She taught other women in the refugee camp how to sew, thanks to a sewing machine donated by people in Torino. Then, in March 1948, she became a mother. Roberto was born at Maria Vittoria, and everyone in the hospital surrounded him with affection and nicknamed him 'the little Pole'. In September, the Canadian government offered her husband a job, and the family crossed the ocean. In her heart and in her mind, she carried the memory of the great compassion of the Italians, and of the Torinese in particular. But destiny did not permit Judith Rubinstein to return to Italy.

A year ago, by chance, in a library in Toronto, she came across a book of lager experiences written by a woman who had been in Auschwitz at the same time as her. She found out that she was now living in Genova. The two women established contact through correspondence, and Judith promised to revisit Italy after an interval of 48 years. And this is how she comes to be here. Upon departing from Genova with her "Torinese" son and her daughter-in-law, Judith Rubinstein wanted to return to Grugliasco to relive one last time the emotions of almost half a century ago.

Appendix B

The following is the original English text of the interview that served as the lead item in the February 2005 issue of Ha-Keillah, *the bi-monthly publication of the Jewish Studies Group of Torino.*

From Torino to Toronto

Interview with Robert Eli Rubinstein

HK: Can you tell us how and why you were born at Grugliasco?

RER: Both of my parents survived the Holocaust but lost most of their family members to the Nazi gas chambers. The only thing my father had left after the war was his flour mill, so when he received word that the Communist government was planning to nationalize all private property and seal the borders, he decided that there was no future in Hungary. Together with eight relatives, my parents (not yet married at the time) crossed the border illegally into Yugoslavia, thereby becoming refugees. Their intention was to run the British blockade and settle in *Eretz Yisrael*. They heard that *hachsharot* (preparatory camps) for this purpose had been established in northern Italy, and so they made their way to Milano. Once there, they were sent to the displaced persons' camp in Grugliasco. They lived there from April 1946 to September 1948, at which time they departed to Canada. I was born on March 5, 1948, not in Grugliasco, which had no maternity facilities, but at the Maria Vittoria Hospital in Torino.

HK: When you were a child, how did your parents tell you about the time you spent at Grugliasco?

RER: My father never speaks about his life before arriving in Canada: this is his way of dealing with the trauma of his horrific wartime experiences. My mother more than compensates for him, however. Before I made contact with Sara Vinçon, my mother was my sole source of information about life in the DP camp. While I was growing up, she always found opportunities to tell me stories about Grugliasco because she believed it was important for me to know about it. She looks back at the involuntary sojourn there in extremely positive terms. She sees the DP camp as a sort of sanatorium where she and all the others could recuperate from the terrible torments they had endured. They had been demoralized by their encounter with human beings at their absolute worst, and they despaired of the future of humanity. As my mother has it, in Grugliasco the Jewish refugees met many ordinary Italians who were warm, compassionate, and generous people. This experience impressed upon them that not all human beings are Jew-murdering Nazis. In time, they were able to regain their faith in humanity, and they began, ever so tentatively, to think optimistically about the future. After nearly three years, they were sufficiently healed that they were ready to go out into the world and rebuild their shattered lives.

HK: We know that you first came back with your mother in June 1996 and then returned a second time at the end of 2004 with your wife and son. What led your mother to go back to Grugliasco?

RER: The first visit was in April 1994. My wife and I were going to a *Bar Mitzvah* of family friends in Milano. My mother had recently established contact with Liana Millu of Genova. After reading Liana's book about her experiences in Auschwitz, my mother realized that they had been there at the same time and in close proximity, and she was eager to meet her. I suggested that she come with us to the *Bar Mitzvah*, and we could travel the triangle of Milano, Genova, and Torino. It was actually my idea to look for the site of the DP camp in Grugliasco. Because of my mother's stories, I was curious to see with my own eyes the place where I started life. No one else in the family had ever expressed interest in this subject, and we had no idea what, if anything, we would find. We were astonished to discover that the site had reverted to its originally designed function as a psychiatric hospital. It was very emotional for my mother to see once again after so many years the place that had been her home during a crucial turning point in her life. As she told the staff we met in the hospital, she was returning to Grugliasco *per dire grazie* (to say thank-you) to the Italian people for helping her in her rehabilitation as a human being.

HK: What does Grugliasco mean to you?

RER: I have internalized the essence of my mother's view that Grugliasco was a crucial way station on my family's journey from despair to hope, a necessary prelude to their successful building of a new life in Canada. For this, I am forever grateful. However, unlike my mother, having been blessedly spared her horrific primary experiences, I have no need to romanticize either the place or the people. The Grugliasco camp was actually a rather dreadful place to live, and a great many Italians have plenty to be ashamed of when it comes to their prewar and wartime behavior, specifically with regard to the Jews in their midst. Perhaps the kindness shown to the refugees after the War was a return to the norms of behavior of a fundamentally civilized people. Perhaps it was the collective expression of a great many guilty consciences. Or perhaps my mother unwittingly exaggerated the positive attributes of Italians as a whole out of a desperate need to believe in the redeemability of humankind.

HK: How did you feel during your two visits? What were the main differences between the first and second visit?

RER: It was a deeply moving experience both times to reconnect with my origins, but in different ways. The first time, I had no idea whether any trace was even left of the camp, as no one had ever inquired about it since 1948, and I knew not a single soul in the vicinity. The second time, I knew exactly what I would find, and I had developed a whole web of contacts. I was particularly touched to discover the Torino Jewish community, of whose existence I had not previously been aware. I found myself thinking that this would have been my own community, had my parents been able to stay in Italy and not immigrated to Canada.

HK: Can you tell us how you ended up in Canada and how you settled in that country?

RER: Staying in Italy was not an option for my parents, both because of the large number of refugees at the time and because of the desperate postwar economic crisis. After almost three years of stagnating in Grugliasco, they were anxious to go anywhere in the world where they could live a normal, dignified life. They wanted to go to *Eretz Yisrael*, but the British blockade made it difficult and dangerous to get through. They patiently waited their turn to disappear in the middle of the night and board a boat in Genova. But by the time the State of Israel was proclaimed, I had just been born, and my parents were not anxious to take their baby into a war zone after all they had been through. In the meantime, a delegation from the heavily Jewish Canadian Fur Workers' Union arrived in Italy to recruit experienced fur workers. In actuality, this was a humanitarian mission to bring as many Jewish refugees as possible to Canada at a time when Canadian immigration policy was blatantly and shockingly anti-Semitic. My father, uncle, and cousin were all accepted by the delegation, although none of them had ever touched a fur. Under the terms of their contract with the government, they were obliged to work as furriers for one year. As soon as the year was up, the three men opened their own fur shop in downtown Toronto. Shortly afterwards, they started building houses, about which they knew even less than they knew about furs. They went on to establish H&R Developments, a large and highly respected real estate development firm in Canada.

HK: Please tell us something about the Jewish community in Canada in general and especially about the one in Toronto.

RER: There are about 360,000 Jews in Canada. Of these, 180,000 live in Toronto, 90,000 in Montreal, and the rest are scattered across the country in smaller communities. In keeping with the global trend, the smaller centers are gradually disappearing, and Jewish life is being consolidated in the major centers. When my family arrived in Toronto in 1948, there were only about 60,000 Jews living there. The Jewish population has exploded in step with the extremely dynamic growth of the city in recent decades. Toronto is a multicultural city consisting mostly of immigrants. By the way, the largest ethnic group in Toronto after the original English inhabitants is the Italians who came in the fifties looking for work. I am fascinated by the fact that they were employed mostly as construction workers, largely by Jewish immigrant builders like my father. Working together, the Italians and the Jews have built Toronto into a great city. From my personal perspective, I see some sort of poetic justice here.

Because so many of the Jews in Toronto are of the first generation in Canada, they tend to have a much stronger Jewish identity than their counterparts in large cities in the United States, who have mostly lived there for many generations and are therefore much more assimilated. An atypically high proportion is religiously observant. We even have quite a few ultra-Orthodox and Hasidim. For a similar reason, the Jewish community of Toronto is one of the most strongly Zionist in the world. Many members have made *aliya* (moved to Israel), including my own daughter Tamar and her family. The Toronto Jewish community is quite affluent overall, but more importantly, it is highly philanthropic. There is a wonderful range of Jewish institutions such as schools, synagogues, community centers, and the world-renowned Baycrest Center for Geriatric Care.

In short, Toronto is a wonderful place to live, and a wonderful place to live as a Jew. Except for the climate: no one I know chooses to live in Toronto because of the climate.

Sometimes things just happen to work out for the best, not a trifling matter considering my parents' history and the blind circumstances that brought them here. Yet, although it is in so many respects a much longer way from Toronto to Torino than the similarity in the names would indicate, my birthplace will always hold a special place in my heart. I look forward to maintaining and deepening my relationship with the Jewish community of Torino, and I wish my new friends there much success in all their endeavors.

Endnotes

Choosing Life

1. Primo Levi, *The Drowned and the Saved* (New York: Summit Books, 1988) p. 82

2. Helen Epstein, "The Heirs of the Holocaust", *The New York Times Magazine*, June 19, 1977, pp. 12-15, 74-77

3. Helen Epstein, *Children of the Holocaust: Conversations with Sons and Daughters of Survivors* (New York: G.P. Putnam's Sons, 1979)

4. Levi, p. 23

Judit

1. Adapted from a story by Judith Rubinstein published on the Internet. *Women and the Holocaust: Personal Reflections* www3.sympatico.ca/mighty1/personal/Judith.htm

2. Randolph L. Braham, *The Politics of Genocide: The Holocaust in Hungary,* Vol. I (New York: Columbia University Press, 1981)

Grugliasco

1. As it turned out, there had indeed been a *mikvah* in the synagogue of Torino, but it was severely damaged by American aerial bombardment towards the end of the War. The Torino *mikvah* was rendered functional again only in 1951.

Torino/Toronto

1. Irving Abella and Harold Troper, *None Is Too Many: Canada and the Jews of Europe, 1933-1948* (Toronto: Lester & Orpen Dennys, 1982)

2. Canada, *House of Commons Debates*, May 1, 1947, 2673-2675.

3. Abella and Troper, p. 8

4. Ibid.

5. Ontario Jewish Archives, MG2 F1a F, file 38, p. 15

6. Ontario Jewish Archives, Regional Executive Minutes File #11a, RG 200, Box 2. UJWF and CJC executive meeting of Aug. 17, 1948.

7. Ontario Jewish Archives, General Correspondence File #756. RG 294, Box 5. Undated article from the *Toronto Telegram* newspaper.

Furs and Mortar

1. See for example: Ontario Jewish Archives, RG 291, Box 2 (17), Toronto Program and Report on Payroll Deduction Plan

2. Ibid. RG 200, Box 2 (11b). C.J.C. Regional Executive meeting minutes, Nov. 10, 1948

3. Ibid. MG 2, I1a, A1, Box 1 (21). Minutes of Board of Directors Meeting Held on December 7, 1948

4. Ibid. RG 294, Box 5, Publicity File 745. No date or radio station identified.

A People Like All Others

1. Exod. 23:9

Confronting the Past

1. Liana Millu, *Smoke Over Birkenau* (Philadelphia: Jewish Publication Society of America, 1991)

2. Gino Li Veli, *Dal Canada per dire 'grazie': Ebrea ungherese ritorna a Grugliasco* (From Canada to say 'thank-you': Hungarian Jewess returns to Grugliasco) in *La Repubblica*, April 15, 1994, p. 3. See Appendix A for an English translation of the article.

In Search of the *Piccolo Polacchino*

1. E-mail of July 15, 2002

2. Massimo Moraglio, *Costruire il manicomio: Storia dell'ospedale psichiatrico di Grugliasco* (Milano: Edizioni Unicopli, 2002) p. 141. My translation from the Italian.

3. E-mail from Sara Vinçon, June 17, 2004

4. *#964- Rubinstein Elia Mordechai di Dov e Schwartz Judith, nato a Torino, Ospedale Maria Vittoria, il 5 Marzo 1948, ore 17:00, circonciso ivi il 12 Marzo 1948 (sabato) dal Prof. Dott. Giulio Segre. Presente il Rabbino Della Pergola.*

5. *Rubinstein Robert, nato il 5 Marzo 1948 alle ore 19:00, presso l'Ospedale Maria Vittoria, da Schwarcz Judith, di anni 27, di professione sarta, cittadina Ungherese, residente a Grugliasco, sposata a Rubinstein Bela, di anni 38, di professione mugnaio, cittadino Ungherese, residente a Grugliasco.*

6. E-mail from Sara Vinçon, July 14, 2004

7. E-mail from Sara Vinçon, November 16, 2005

8. See Appendix B.

9. Sara Vinçon, *Vite in transito: La storia del campo profughi di Grugliasco (1945-1949)* Tesi di Laurea, Universita Degli Studi di Torino, Facolta di Lettere e Filosofia, Corso di Laurea in Storia

How It Really Was

1. A pseudonym

Keeping Faith

1. She committed it to writing in 2001, and it was subsequently posted on a web site featuring stories by survivors living in Toronto. See www3.sympatico.ca/mighty1/personal/**judith**2.htm

2. Mark Mandelbaum, ed., *Hofstedter Family Chronicles,* (Toronto, Private publication, 1992) p. 256

Onward

1. Literally, "in the sanctification of God's name." Jewish tradition reserves this phrase for those who are put to death because they are Jews.

2. The Jewish calendar equivalent of August 20, 2007.

R obert Eli Rubinstein, the son of Holocaust survivors from Hungary, was born in Torino, Italy, in 1948 while his parents were trapped in a nearby refugee camp. Arriving in Canada with his parents as an infant, he was raised and educated in Toronto. Mr. Rubinstein is a real-estate developer and communal leader. He and his wife Renée, also a child of survivors, have four children and eight grandchildren.